Study Time Management

Lynn Underwood

Edited by Lin Wilkinson

foulsham

London • New York • Toronto • Sydney

foulsham

The Publishing House, Bennetts Close,
Cippenham, Berkshire, SL1 5AP, England.

ISBN 0-572-02185-2

Typeset by Imaging Design Services

Printed in Great Britain by St. Edmundsbury Press, Bury St Edmunds, Suffolk

Contents

Introduction

If you are embarking on A levels, moving into higher education or returning to study after years working or bringing up a family, the task ahead may look daunting.

It's certainly challenging, but don't despair. Your overriding objective should be to enjoy your studies by organising them effectively, making your life as easy as possible, and so achieve the success you're aiming for. Why else would you do it?

Studying is something most people regard with dread. When you are at school you have to do it; later in life you choose to do it. Few people are blessed with a genuine love of studying *per se*. Most will find something in their course programme which is tedious, difficult to grasp, indigestible or just plain boring, but it has to be done to achieve that final qualification.

The art (or science, or discipline) of studying effectively is rarely something that comes naturally. It may be much easier when you are young and transferring from school to a higher education programme. But even then it can have its problems. Higher education requires a much greater degree of self-reliance and self-motivation. There is no pressure from lecturers to force the pace. There may be some peer pressure from fellow students, but whether you respond to the challenge is up to you. Studying effectively and accumulating knowledge is entirely your decision. Someone else can take your place if you fail. And after all, success is the goal.

Later in life, after years away from study because of family or work commitments, it can be much harder to tackle, particularly if you are trying to study part-time around the demands of a job and/or a family.

Very much later in life, when all such pressures are gone, studying can be a joy – a luxury – a way of keeping one's brain active and preventing a stagnant old age. When there is no pressure to gain qualifications to earn a living or improve your lot in life, you can study for the sheer pleasure of it.

This book can help to make your life easier. It will help you to organise your study effectively, from the basics of where you work, to when and how you work, with advice on time management, research, note-taking, and management and storage of information. It provides advice on written assignments, ways of improving your memory, and strategies for coping successfully with revision and examinations.

By learning to study effectively you will be acquiring new skills which will help you in all aspects of life. The ability to analyse information and extract relevant facts, to manage your time effectively and to get to know yourself sufficiently well that you know how much work you can cope with at any given time, will all be drawn upon after you finish your period of study and are making your way in the world in whatever capacity.

Developing self-discipline can be a great asset in any area of life. Learning to study effectively is an excellent way to start.

1 Study with Attitude

Your attitude to your studies and above all your motivation are crucial to the enjoyment you derive and to your eventual success.

Choose your course carefully

The course you decide upon is of paramount importance. Do as much research as you can before making your choice – read prospectuses carefully, visit colleges, talk to tutors and to students already taking similar courses. It will be very difficult to succeed if you do not enjoy and feel stimulated by the course you choose, and that will affect your motivation. This book will help you to determine why you are setting out on a course of study and what you hope to gain from it.

Decide if you wish to study at a college or university or through distance learning. Ensure that you are the sort of person who can work in isolation from others before you opt for distance learning (see Chapter 5).

Motivation: why do I want to do this?

You must be absolutely clear why you are setting out on these studies. What are your goals? Are you embarking on this course of study:

- for personal satisfaction?
- to get your brain moving after years away from study?
- to catch up on education you missed the 'first time around'?
- to gain a specific qualification?

- for career advancement?

- for a better job and/or more money?

- for educational advancement?

A former student I knew stuck a big notice above his desk and looked at it every day. It said 'The only way I am going to get out of Salford is by getting a degree'. Now this may be a bit unfair to Salford, but it was the motivation for this individual to gain an honours degree and move to America.

Make a list of your own reasons for undertaking your course of study. These may be:

- I'm bored witless just being a housewife and want to use my brain.

- I don't want to stay in the same job for the rest of my life.

- I want to earn more money and provide my children with a better life.

- I want to give myself the best possible chance of getting a good job when I leave university.

- I want to learn something new now that I have retired.

- I want to be able to travel the world and use my new skills.

- I want to prove that just because I'm disabled doesn't mean that I'm not as capable as the next person.

You get the idea. You have to keep reminding yourself why you are doing what you are doing.

Unfortunately, a lot of young students go on to higher education because they can't think of anything better to do after they leave school. This is not a promising start. *Motivation is everything*. It separates the good from the indifferent.

Sometimes parents don't help. They put an unnecessary burden of guilt on young people by using phrases like 'Don't you want us to be proud of you?' or 'I hope you realise how much your education is costing us?' Motivation is not gained by bullying, which only causes resentment.

Motivation has to be self-generated. Someone else may unwittingly impart it to you by, say, generating a sense of competition. Wanting to be better than someone else is not harmful as long as you concentrate your efforts on yourself and not on 'doing down' the person with whom you are competing. Motivation can also be generated through a sense of pride – not wishing to be less than others, or wanting to show off your capabilities. Amongst students a sense of pride is good, which is why many educators encourage group activities and projects. Teamwork generates a strong sense of pride and competitiveness. Shared study groups can be a way of organising your own team activities. This is discussed in Chapter 6.

Never lose sight of your objectives

Re-evaluate them from time to time and make sure they still apply. If not, why not?

Embarking upon A levels or higher education involves very hard work, but enormous pleasure and benefits can be gained. Your views may change as you progress through your course, and you may emerge a very different person. So don't be afraid of re-evaluating your aims and objectives from time to time, and make sure they still apply. Ask yourself honestly:

- have I changed?
- has my attitude towards studies changed?
- are my goals still meaningful?
- do I need to alter some of my goals?

Be honest – the demands will be great

Pre-course analysis is crucial. Can you cope with the demands of a job, family and other commitments *and* study? Draw up a realistic map of your time and commitments and honestly analyse whether, after you have reallocated some of your tasks to others and eliminated others, you have enough time to study without damaging your quality of life, your health or your relationships.

Organise Your Way to Success

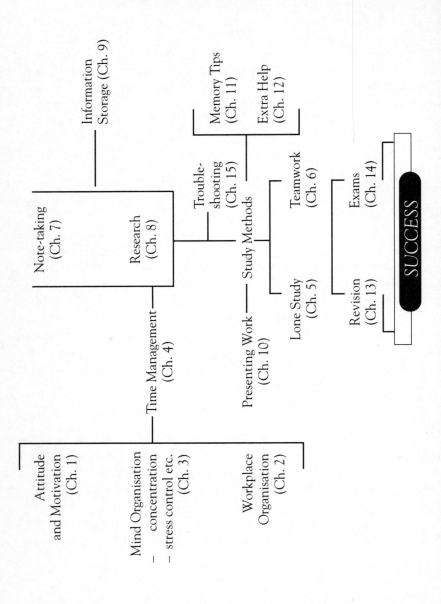

2 Sort Out the Basics

The key to an effective study programme is organisation – a system for managing yourself, your time, your resources, your study material and your thoughts.

The alternative is disarray, lack of direction, lack of time and ultimately panic, because you cannot pull everything together in time for those vital assignments, assessments or exams.

Tools of the trade

In order to study effectively you need the basic requirements – a place to study, time to study, pens, pencils, rulers, paper, notebooks, files, and these days almost certainly a computer and disks. Some people are so disorganised they waste at least half an hour every time they plan to study by searching for the basics they need.

So, make sure you have two sets of the basics. You can't, unless you are very lucky, have two computers (one portable!), but you can carry around with you one set of the essentials, and keep one set at home. If you are highly organised, like one student I know, you'll carry a bag of pens, pencils, mathematical instruments, note pads, an empty carrier bag (for carrying away books he may withdraw from the library), a handful of 10p coins (for photocopying), a small stapler and a box of spare staples. We may not all be that organised, but it's worth a try!

A place to study

Above all you need a place to study – a place where you can keep your files and have most of your resources to hand, where you will have quiet and no distractions, and where you can concentrate on difficult tasks without too much interruption.

Of course, you can study in a library, in a room at college, on a train or on the kitchen table, but these have severe limitations. Most libraries close by 8 p.m. at the latest, and do not open again until 9 a.m. at the earliest. Most colleges have 100 students fighting for time in a small study room, if indeed, such a luxury is available. The train may be fine for reading but not for writing – what if you can't get a seat? The kitchen table may be all right if it's the only room in the house where you are left alone, but it's not ideal.

Studying at home is the same as running a business from home. Ideally you need a room, or at least part of a room, which is specifically for that purpose and nothing else.

You should have all your files and books to hand, along with your computer, writing materials and so on. You should be able to break off from what you are doing, and be able to leave it, untouched, until you come back to it. Having to gather up all your materials and transport them from place to place is a waste of effort and time. It will also lead to confusion and lack of organisation, and important things will be mislaid. If you only have a precious hour in which to study, you don't want to waste half of it setting things out and clearing them away again.

3   Get Your Mind Into Gear

You have decided upon a course of study. That was the easy part! Now you need to focus your mind, so you make your studies as stress-free, enjoyable and effective as you can. Then you can turn the choice you've made into a solid and rewarding achievement. Remember, this is all about making your life easier and achieving the success you're aiming for.

This is where you take self-discipline on to a higher plane. Overcoming any natural tendency to laziness, or disinterest, boredom, frustration, lack of understanding, periods of ill-health, tiredness and a general desire to be doing something else, at times will require a supreme effort. If you're working and/or caring for a family as well as studying, the effort and commitment needed will be all the greater.

Stress: learn to manage it

First a word about that disease of the twentieth century – stress. We all suffer from it, to some degree. It seems to be unavoidable. Life today is full of pressure because demands are greater. We are expected to cram far more into our days than our forebears ever did. We expect more of ourselves. We want to travel further, learn more, have more material possessions and get more out of life than our parents or grandparents did. For many women the role of housewife and mother is no longer enough, even supposing we all had a choice and were not dictated to by economic necessity. Staying in the same job for 20 years is considered unambitious, even if industry and commerce were stable enough to offer such a luxury.

There are periods in life, however, when we need to 'tread water', to minimise the pressures in order to achieve greater things later on. A concentrated period of study is one such period. You have consciously to decide to reduce your level of stress while you are studying. There will be time enough when studying is finished to join the rat race again.

Methods of organisation and time management discussed in the next chapter are steps towards minimising stress. Allowing yourself time to complete your tasks, seeking co-operation from others to help you complete those tasks and organising your surroundings and resources so they are conducive to effective work means that you remove the pressure that comes from not knowing when or where or how you are going to complete your current workload. Freedom from those worries is a step in the right direction.

Differentiate between good stress and bad stress

Good stress is when you feel a surge of adrenaline as you face a challenge with confidence. It is pressure, but it shouldn't be a source of anxiety or depression. This is how you should face up to exams. They should be a 'good stress' experience, and the key lies in the level of confidence you feel.

Bad stress is when you struggle through a course of study, staggering from one assignment to the next, with no confidence, and with pressure and anxiety mounting.

Have you chosen the right course?

The importance of choosing the right course was emphasised in Chapter 1. Many students, both full- and part-time, find that the course they choose is not what they expected and feel forced to pull out after a time. It goes without saying that, before you start your studies, you must fully understand what the course content will be, where your strengths and weaknesses lie, whether you will be able to overcome them with extra help. For example, many degree courses today contain some business administration. Students interested in a subject like home economics may not realise that their course will contain a hefty section on accounting, because the prime aim of educators is to send students into the hard-headed world of food retailing. Anyone with a poor grasp of arithmetic may find this part of the course extremely stressful. You should discuss such concerns at length before you embark on the course. You must ask questions. Are there alternative courses? If not, is extra tuition available for problematic subjects?

Always communicate

Once you have started your course, make sure you and your lecturers communicate clearly. Bad stress comes from a lack of understanding. If you are faced with an assignment you do not fully understand, it will only cause you anxiety. You must ask questions, whether you are on a traditional course or studying by correspondence. If your questions are met with irritation, complain. Educators are paid to communicate their subject matter. It is not your fault if they are bad communicators. Your needs matter.

This does not mean that you should be a pest and irritate other students by constantly interrupting a lecture. Make a note of all your questions and talk to the lecturer afterwards.

Think positive

Stress through lack of confidence can come from the realisation that other students on the course know more about the subject matter than you do, perhaps because they may have touched on it before on another course, such as A level. Take this in your stride. Do not allow self-doubt to creep in, or it will paralyse your private study. Think, for example, of other students who are doing a course in what may be their second language. If they can cope, so can you.

Self-doubt is the greatest enemy if you are trying, for the most part, to study alone, either by correspondence, through the Open University or for an external degree. It can sometimes be easy to lapse into negative thinking when you are working in a vacuum and are unable to discuss the quality of your work on a regular basis. This can be overcome. More about that in Chapter 5.

Positive thinking should always be your goal. If you have organised yourself and your time and you understand the course content, this should be easy, because you can continually say to yourself 'I know I can do this. There are no obstacles. I just have to concentrate my time and efforts'.

Eliminate uncertainty

Being unsure about whether your computer is reliable, whether you can get to and from college without a car, whether your accommodation is going to be available next term – all these things add to your bad stress level.

Do not just hope they will sort themselves out. Get the computer looked at, the car serviced, find out about alternative methods of transport, and get your living accommodation sorted out.

Students who have to think about the arrangements of others as well as themselves, if they have a family, for instance, need to get those sorted out too. Who is going to pick the children up from school if you have a lecture? Who is going to take your daughter to Brownies on the evening you have a class scheduled?

Aim for peace of mind from the outset. You cannot concentrate on your studies if you are worried about minor problems.

Concentrate, concentrate

The great enemy of effective study is lack of concentration. Distractions, tiredness and boredom are all factors that destroy concentration.

In Chapter 2 we discussed organising a quiet place to study and the time to study, and communicating your needs to others so that as many distractions as possible are removed.

Of course there will be unseen distractions that only you can deal with – personal relationships may occupy more of your thoughts than you care to admit; the offer of a fun night out which you have refused but which keeps beckoning, may destroy your ability to concentrate; you may have a nagging feeling of guilt that you should be doing something else, like washing clothes, cleaning your home or helping the kids with their homework, rather than studying.

Very few people are so single-minded that they can push the rest of the world to one side and concentrate totally on what they want to do. Those that are may become multi-millionaires but are probably not very likeable people. Most of us are prey to common feelings and desires that frequently interrupt our concentration. However, you have to recognise when these distractions are getting out of hand. The single-mindedness of those potential millionaires is born out of one thing – motivation. Find your motivation and make it the creed by which you channel your powers of concentration to the task in hand.

Set yourself study goals – and rewards

Setting yourself study goals is a good way to raise your standards and achieve a sense of fulfilment. Some are already set for you, of course. You have study assignments, projects and examinations. But these are only primary targets. Of course you have to fulfil these tasks, but do you want to do them well? Nudging up the quality of your work is a game you can play with yourself. Set targets of excellence and promise yourself rewards if you achieve them.

Try this checklist:

Goals:

I will get a B grade for my next paper.

I will find some interesting new material to inject into my next project.

I will meticulously map out my next essay and give myself plenty of time not only to write it but also to edit it and rewrite it if necessary.

I will start a programme of continuous revision by tackling a particular topic in depth every month.

I will make greater efforts to improve the quality of my research material.

Rewards:

If I get a B grade for my next paper I will celebrate by taking my friend/spouse/flatmate out for dinner.

If I find some interesting new material for my next project I will buy myself that new jumper/tennis racquet/videotape/CD.

If I am satisfied that I have really worked hard on my next essay I will take two days off and visit home/friends/the beach.

If I keep up my continuous revision programme I will have a good holiday in the summer.

If I improve the quality of my research material I will buy those concert tickets/theatre tickets/train tickets.

Of course, if you improve the quality of your work by meeting your study goals you will get other rewards too – praise from your tutors, admiration of friends and family, and so on. But it is the goals and rewards that you set yourself that really count. It is a form of self-love, but it has to be a 'tough love'. You have to push yourself to meet your goals, and only then can you reward yourself. It is a refinement of motivation. Even if you have other motivations for working, reward yourself too. You cannot have too much motivation!

Fear of failure: face it head on

Sometimes people have such a lack of self-confidence that their whole lives are dominated by a fear of failure which prevents them undertaking any challenges, however small. Or one instance of failure during a course of study has a knock-on effect and can make them afraid to take up any more challenges.

If this is a problem talk it through with someone else, family or friends or even, in extreme cases, your doctor. Start by writing down all your anxieties. Sometimes when things are written down they slide into perspective, and you can start a discussion with yourself about how foolish some of your fears actually are.

Let's take an example:

Question

I got a very low mark for my last paper and I am frightened of getting one again. Why did I get a low mark?

Answer

Because I didn't understand the subject matter very well.

Question

Why didn't I ask for help?

Answer

Because I thought I would look stupid.

Question

Didn't my tutor think I was stupid for turning in such a poor paper?

Answer

Yes. He said so.

Question

Do I think he would have respected me for asking more questions before I did the paper?

Answer

Probably. He always says he's there to help.

Question

Is there any reason why I should make the same mistake again?

Answer

No.

This simple exercise has eliminated one fear, just by working it through. Although this may seem rather contrived, it is a good way of working through a fear sufficiently to be able to take it to the next step – talking to someone about it. In the example, the student may have locked the fear and embarrassment over that one failure into themselves to such a degree that they couldn't talk to their tutor about it. This exercise should rationalise the fear sufficiently for the student to be able to confirm the findings by having a similar conversation face to face with the tutor in question.

If you are working alone at home, have a reassuring conversation with a relative or friend. You cannot work in a vacuum. You have to be able to use others as a sounding board. If you're contemplating studying at home make sure you start with the full support and understanding of family and friends, otherwise you will find the task very hard indeed. You have to feel that someone is taking an interest in what you are doing, although not in the fine detail, of course. Losing perspective because of isolation can lead to all kinds of psychological problems.

Learn to pace yourself

Tiredness and lack of relaxation can really hamper studies if they are not dealt with.

The heady sense of freedom and 'adulthood' that all undergraduates experience when they first leave home has to be worked through. Burning the candle at both ends is something only the very young can deal with, and then only for a limited time. Even they will eventually succumb to exhaustion and ill-health if they do not learn to pace themselves, and those who do not realise this are most at risk of falling into the trap of using 'stimulants' to get them through important study periods and examinations. It is to be hoped that most young people today appreciate the foolishness of going down that path, but it does not hurt to repeat the warning.

If you are a young student you might push yourself too hard in the pursuit of pleasure, but older students can also be at risk from trying to do too much in too many areas of their lives.

Recognise your limitations

We all have different tolerances. What may be a source of anxiety to you will not be to someone else. Some people do not need as much sleep as others. Some people are quite happy working in chaotic surroundings. However, most people function far more effectively if they work with a sense of calm and security and with a degree of energy.

Get to know your own limitations. Perhaps you can manage with less sleep and more fun at the weekends, and be stricter with yourself during the week. Good food, sleep and some fun will make studying much less of a chore!

Coping with illness

Pacing yourself includes making allowances for periods of illness. You may be fortunate enough to be fit, healthy and active and bouts of illness may be few. Or you may have problems that frequently recur. These can range from periods which incapacitate you every month, to a lifelong struggle with a serious illness or a physical disability which you know will diminish your energy and your ability to concentrate from time to time. In these cases you have to work as much as you can when you have the energy and ability to do so. Tackle the big projects and the difficult essays when you are energised and save the reading and the lighter work for when you are below par.

Of course, periods of illness do not always come along when it is convenient, but if you work to the rule of doing as much as you can today and not put it off until tomorrow you will be able to take advantage of good health most of the time.

Boredom: just grit your teeth...

Imagine yourself in this situation: you hate the particular subject matter you are faced with. You find this particular part of your course the most boring. You cannot concentrate on it because it is so uninteresting.

There is no advice to offer here other than to summon up all your motivation techniques, grit your teeth and get on with it. The sooner you do, the sooner it is finished.

Studying is supposed to be an exercise that prepares you for life in the real world. Life is often boring, irritating, uninteresting, stressful, time-consuming and full of problems, but we have to work through it and come out the other side. If you throw in the towel over a boring assignment on a trivial subject, how can you ever cope with the really unavoidable things in life? Sometimes, life is a bitch. Give yourself a really big reward when you have struggled through and overcome this difficult patch.

Learn to say 'no'

You can only take on so many commitments in life. Learn to say 'no' to those extra requests that will just take you over the edge and leave you unable to cope. For example, if you are trying to hold down a job, be part of a family and study, you can't put yourself up as a local councillor, however flattering it may be to be asked or however much you may want to do so. There is a limit to how much you can fit into your life. There will be another opportunity.

Saying 'yes' to yet another party invitation, when you know you only have the weekend in which to complete an important paper, is crazy. You only have one opportunity to complete your studies. After that you can party for the rest of your life if you want to!

When you have a family to consider, saying 'no' is often very hard. You do not want to deny your children the pleasures of childhood for the sake of your study. Be reasonable. If the demand is reasonable you have to go along with it and find some way of working around it. If the demand is unreasonable, such as 'Mum, can I have my German pen pal over to stay for two weeks?' and it just happens to coincide with your examination period, then say 'no', but offer an alternative. The family has to learn to set priorities just as you do.

Cut out the negative

Is there ever a right time to study? Probably not, if you are going to sit down and list all the reasons why you shouldn't be doing it. Negative thinking only leads to inactivity. There is no point in approaching every day saying 'I can't study today, I've got a headache/I'm bored with studying/I didn't sleep enough last night/I don't feel like it'. Don't allow others to be negative or encourage you to be negative. The husband who continually says 'I don't know what you want to do all this studying for' needs to be told firmly to either back you up or shut up. The friends who try to encourage you to abandon your studying, even if it is only for one day, are like people who try to encourage alcoholics to have more fun and take a drink – they are not friends worth having. Teach those around you to value what you are doing as much as you value it yourself.

So be positive. Take a headache pill/read your motivation motto/get some more sleep/get working.

The thirteen commandments

Here is a checklist to help you make those study periods positive:

- Get a good night's sleep
- Eat regularly and properly
- Find out what motivates you to succeed
- Set yourself some targets
- Promise yourself some rewards
- Do as much as you can while you have the energy
- Eliminate unnecessary stress in your life
- Organise your study place/time and methods

- Give yourself time to study and time to relax

- Analyse any anxieties you may have and talk them through with someone

- Try to build up your confidence by acquiring knowledge, developing a sense of security, and through success in achievements

- Know yourself, your body and your commitments so that if you begin to be overloaded you can pull back and give yourself a recovery period

- Organise support from family, friends and flatmates – both physical and psychological.

Case histories

The case histories illustrate some problems that can occur, and solutions that have been found.

Case 1

The problem

David is a manager in his mid-thirties with a wife and two small children. He decided to do an MBA in order to advance his career. This involved studying at night and at weekends. He also commuted daily to a fairly demanding job which necessitated leaving home at 6 a.m. and returning at 7 p.m. As both his children are under five, they sometimes wake during the night and are subject to frequent common childhood ailments, which they pass on to the rest of the family. David is therefore operating on a knife-edge, brought about by overwork, interrupted sleep, frequent colds and coughs and lack of relaxation. He is increasingly unable to keep up with his course content.

The solution

He has finally decided to postpone his MBA studies until the children are both at school.

Case 2

The problem

Sandra is a full-time single mother of an eight-year-old and is desperate to achieve a qualification which will enable her to run her own business from home. She is therefore attending two daytime classes and one evening class locally. However, she has no help in the home. On occasion she has had to miss classes because her baby-sitter has let her down, and she is constantly beset by feelings of guilt that she is neglecting to spend quality time with her child. This has led to difficulties in sleeping and a constant state of anxiety.

The solution

Her solution, after discussion with her tutor at the local college, has been to switch to a correspondence course. Although she misses the company of other students, it has given her more flexibility and she feels more relaxed.

Case 3

The problem

Daniel is a full-time student at a university in the north of England, some distance away from his home. He is in his second year of studies and has had to move out of the halls of residence where he had a room to himself, as those rooms are reserved for first-year students only. He has moved into a shared flat in the town. His flatmates are not very considerate or organised; they keep irregular hours and do not do their share of domestic work in the flat. Daniel is becoming increasingly irritated by the stress this causes him. His sleep is often interrupted by their comings and goings and he has frequent arguments about the state of their living quarters.

The solution

After consulting with a student counsellor, they came up with a solution. Daniel moved to a bedsit of his own, which is slightly more expensive, but he finances it by doing a Saturday job in a supermarket. Since his life is more stable, he feels better able to concentrate on his studies and can cope better.

4 Make Your Time Work

Now we come to the big one. Time management. Managing your time and, perhaps, the time of others. Here you may have to struggle to overcome your own personality. If you are the sort of person who tends to put off tasks until the very last minute, you are going to have to make superhuman efforts to change your pattern of working. This is serious study. This is not school. Most of today's higher education courses have a built-in continuous assessment structure, and therefore set a level of constant application to work which cannot be avoided.

You have to make the most of the study time you have. This may be much more difficult for some people than for others. If you have to work as well as study, you have less time available for study than students who have the luxury of being able to devote themselves solely to their course. If you have a family to care for, you have additional demands that cannot be avoided.

Again, we come back to organisation. You have to organise yourself first and then organise other people to fit around you. Successful study requires a degree of selfishness (of the nicest possible kind!).

List your commitments

First itemise your time commitments, to discover what free time you have available.

Example: Mary Mitchell

Employment	9 to 5 every weekday
Attendance at lectures	Two weekday evenings a week
Dealing with family	7 to 8 every morning; 6 to 8 every evening; variable at weekends

Mary Mitchell has very little free time available for study. It would seem that she has from 8 p.m. to 10 p.m., say, three evenings a week during the week, for study.

Mary's husband or a friend could take the children out on Saturday afternoons, leaving her free to study. She needs some recreation and time with her family, so let's say she goes out with her husband on Saturday evenings, spends Sundays with the family and studies again on Sunday evenings when the children have gone to bed. She may also, with a bit of organisation, such as taking sandwiches and her essential study tools to work, be able to study in a library near her work place, or at her desk, or in some quiet place, during her lunch breaks.

Here we have a scenario where every moment for study has to be carefully planned, snatched even, from a busy weekly schedule. It does not allow for illness, of herself or her children. The best-laid plans often go by the board when a child is ill, off school and in need of constant comfort and entertainment. These sort of things always seem to happen just when you have an important assignment to complete!

It is not always possible to plan for the unforeseen but you can make sure that you achieve as much as possible, in the time you have available, by setting yourself targets and trying to get ahead of your timescale so that, if the unforeseen does happen and you are prevented from working for a few days, it is not disastrous.

Set priorities

You will find this a useful discipline to have acquired by the time you come to take examinations. The technique is to look at the tasks that need to be undertaken and assess them in order of priority.

The order of priority can be based on different things:

Urgency – something that needs to be done now

Difficulty – something that will take a lot of time to do

Duty – something you have promised will be done by a certain time or date

Routine – something that can be done when you are short of time or capability, i.e. when you have a headache or are very tired, and can only manage something undemanding.

Setting priorities should be part of planning your day. You need to look at your available time and at the demands on your time and attention that are likely to arise throughout the day, and then look at the tasks you need to complete.

Plan your week

If you remember the advice earlier about getting ahead of yourself so that an unforeseen crisis does not badly disrupt your study schedule, you will realise that planning, say, to do an important essay on Thursday night rather than now is laying yourself open to problems. If something crops up on Thursday night that prevents you from doing it, you will have wasted the earlier part of the week and left yourself short of time in which to complete the task.

Let's look at a sample list of tasks:

- Write up notes from last lecture
- Research a particular topic at the library
- Dig out some previous information from journals in the library to photocopy
- Filing
- Essay to be submitted by next week
- Read a section of a textbook for discussion in class next week
- Write to your mother
- Pay some bills
- Make some phone calls.

Now we take each task as listed and analyse its priority level:

Write up notes from last lecture
This should be classified as 'urgent', as notes should always be written up when fresh and when you can remember the background

detail of the lecture, programme or book you have just listened to or read.

Research a particular topic at library
The urgency of this depends upon whether you need the information now or whether it can be put off until later.

Dig out previous information at library and photocopy
The difficulty here may be that the library often only keeps copies of journals for so many months. If you leave this task too long, your opportunity to photocopy the information may be lost.

Filing
This should always be done regularly otherwise you forfeit any good organisation you have built up. However, it is a task that can be fitted in and around, say, making telephone calls.

Essay (to be submitted next week)
Start it now. Do it bit by bit, when you have a spare hour each day. Don't leave it all for a particular day later in the week. Remember the 'unforeseen circumstances' rule.

Read a section of a textbook for discussion next week
This sort of thing can be done each night in bed. Don't waste valuable time during the day on something that does not require maximum creative energy.

Write to your mother
One of the 'duty' tasks perhaps. Again, something that can be done late at night. Any tasks that do not require you to struggle to find words or remember detail can be done when you are tired.

Pay some bills
An 'urgent' task maybe? But one that can be fitted in and around the telephone calls and filing.

Make some phone calls
These may be time-constrained because you can only telephone certain people at certain times. Let us assume you have to call people in the evenings.

Plan your day

If you are a full-time student, you may have lectures all morning and a free afternoon on this particular day. After lunch you can therefore decide to spend several hours applying yourself to the following tasks:

- Writing up notes

- Starting your essay

- Filing.

Then, if you still have time before the library shuts and you need to stretch your legs and have a change of scene, you can go to the library to do your research and photocopying.

Later, in the evening, you can make your phone calls, do some more filing and pay some bills. If you feel alert enough you can do a little more on your essay, then take yourself off to bed, write your letter to your mother and read a few pages of your textbook before going to sleep. Planning the day has made a productive use of your time, energy and resources.

The student with much less time available, for example, one who works full-time or has a family to cope with, has to set different priorities and juggle with the limited time they have available.

Group tasks

One of the most valuable things to do is to group similar tasks together. For example, those that do not require total concentration can be done at a time when other people are present and distraction will not matter. Filing, paying bills, writing letters and making phone calls can all be done with the family present and making the usual interruptions.

Going to the library can double up as a family outing, provided you use one that has a children's section and can offer the children some diversion while you dig out your articles and photocopy them.

Reading set textbooks can be done on the train whilst commuting to work or in bed while you are relaxing before sleep. Writing up notes can also be done on the train.

Plan to use your uninterrupted quiet time, when the family have gone to bed, for serious work that requires your concentration. If one child is going to have tea after school with a friend, try to persuade someone to take the other child as well, so that you can get a couple of uninterrupted hours as a bonus.

Remember: the secret of maximising your useful time is to control it. Look at the tasks you need to do, assess the quality of the time that is needed for the tasks and allot time to them accordingly. Haphazard grabbing of odd moments is not productive and not organised enough for you to achieve your targets.

Set targets

This management technique sounds daunting and you may wonder what place it has in a normal study plan. The answer is that it is really quite a simple concept. We have discussed the basic idea above.

First identify your tasks, then place them in order of priority. Then you have your 'targets'. You know when you have to complete certain tasks and what is required in order for you to complete them. You may be a fortunate full-time student with your own computer and therefore able to achieve your targets without any help from anyone else. However, you may be someone who can only achieve your targets with the co-operation of others.

For example, you may need to negotiate the following:

- *computer time* at the college or from your flatmates with whom you share a computer

- *a study room* at the college or the spare room you share as a study with your flatmates

- *studying time* which you may need to request from your employers or your family

- *research material* which may have to be requested from a library or resource centre; you may have to share time with these materials with other students.

So, in order to achieve your targets you have to explain them to others and hope that your needs can be accommodated within their framework. It requires an element of co-operation between you and the other parties to achieve your targets.

You may be part of a study group in which you are not only setting yourself individual targets but also setting group targets. But more of that in Chapter 6.

Computer time

If you are sharing a computer with other students at college or where you live, borrowing a computer at work or sharing one with your family, you need to communicate with each other to find out how you can best share your resource.

Using a college computer is probably the most difficult, since the competition for time will be fierce. You need to discuss your needs with whoever controls use of the computer and aim to organise a set time or times each week when you can use it. You then have to be disciplined enough to stick rigidly to those times and plan the use of the rest of your time in preparatory work so that your time on the computer is maximised.

Sharing a computer with flatmates can be difficult; some people are not very organised and may just decide to use the computer when they feel like it. You will need to gently suggest that you all draw up a rota based on your individual course requirements and work needs. After all, by now you have learnt to assess your needs, manage your time and set priorities, haven't you? So you can show the others how to do the same. They may grumble, but may thank you in the end when they realise how much more effectively their time is being spent.

Sharing a computer with the family should be easier. If the children need it for their homework they should be finished by 8 p.m. and you can have it after they go to bed. At weekends, you have to assert your parental authority and make sure you get first claim on it.

If you have computer facilities at work, ask the boss if you can use a computer during your lunch hour. Most are amenable, provided you can reassure them that you are not interrupting your own or other people's work, and that you are only using your own virus-free tested disks.

Study room

The same principles apply to the use of a shared room as to a shared computer. Again it is a question of organisation.

If you are sharing a room with flatmates or with the family make sure it is organised properly. Everyone should have their own bookcase/file/shelf/work pending tray etc. Don't let everyone's work material get muddled up. Establish a rule that the desk is cleared after each person has used it and that things are put away. Make sure everyone does their own filing on a regular basis. Treat the room as if it were a shared office.

It needs some discipline on everyone's part if it is to be a useful study area and not a tip which has to be tidied up every time you want to do some work.

Keep things in the same place all the time. It is an enormous waste of energy to have to spend valuable working time looking for essential materials before you can start your important tasks.

Larger libraries have study rooms available, which can be booked, usually at no charge. However, librarians expect you to be reliable and turn up when you have booked a regular slot; there are plenty of people competing for the same resource.

Study time

If after you have organised your time and yourself you still find you haven't enough time to complete your workload, it may be possible to negotiate with your course tutor to see if the workload can be spread, or you can adapt your course to allow you a bit more free time. Don't struggle needlessly. Get it sorted out.

Communication between flatmates is essential if you are to allocate yourselves sufficient study time. Of course, sometimes students who share flats and are on different courses are a bit like ships that pass in the night. Face-to-face communication can sometimes be difficult. If that is the case, stick up a bulletin board and post notes to each other on it. There is nothing worse than planning a quiet night's study to complete an important project, only to find that your flatmate has arranged to have a large dinner party, with laughter and lively discussion going on until the small hours.

Creating study time within a family requires the understanding and co-operation of all family members. If your spouse is agreeable, get him or her to take the children out every Saturday morning to give you some hours of peace. If you are also working, get the children to help with the housework so that when they go to bed you don't have to waste valuable time cleaning the house when you should be studying.

Research materials

Sometimes the books you need to access are so rare or so much in demand that they have to be booked well in advance, and you can only read them *in situ* or have them on loan for a short period. You must build this consideration into your study plan. First find out what you need and then how long the material will take to get; whether you can only use it for reference (i.e. only look at it in the library), or whether you will be able to take it home, and for how long.

You may also require copies of journals which are only held in specialist libraries. This may necessitate ordering photocopies of the articles by post (for which there will be a charge), or you may have to make a special trip to the library in question.

Some libraries and resource centres can only be used by members, or by special application – the Public Records Office, for example, or the Reading Room at the British Museum. Again you must make all the relevant enquiries early on in your study programme so you can build your time management around this.

And finally...

By now, you should be able to see the importance of organisation and time management. It's a bit like dieting; at first it's hard to be disciplined and think through the plan for each day, but after a while it should become second nature. These skills can be carried over into whatever you do after you complete your course of study, and you will find that this self-discipline will be of benefit to you, your family and your future employers.

5   How to Study: working alone

There are millions of people, all over the world, who study completely alone – by correspondence course, by radio, purely from books, or who take external degrees, or, in Britain, do Open University courses. In fact, because of the vast size of some countries, like Australia, children study alone from the age of five, with just the aid of a radio or television to supplement their books.

Many adults study alone because they are housebound or cannot afford the time to study at a college. Studying alone requires a high degree of self-reliance and self-discipline, but millions have successfully completed studies and not gone mad in the process!

Home alone – good or bad?

Distance education, as it is called, has been available to students for well over 100 years and its advantages and disadvantages have been extensively researched and documented. Dave Stewart (Open University, UK) has written several books on the subject, based on his extensive experience, and he lists the advantages of distance learning as:

Freedom from the 'straitjacket of the lecture hall'

You do not have to learn to a timetable, spend time attending lectures or devote time to other college activities. You can spend what time you have available purely on study.

Ability to study whenever and wherever you desire

Exactly that. The student studying at home can choose, within reason, the time and place of study.

Freedom inherent in the individuality of the distance student's situation

There is a great sense of freedom in being your own master, without interference, as long as you do not abuse that freedom by failing to stick to the targets and schedules you have set yourself.

Student not bound by the learning pattern of a learning group

You can learn by your own methods, however unorthodox, and can work at your own pace, which may be faster than a group would allow.

A distance student's needs are not subservient to the needs of a learning group

You do not have to consider anyone but yourself and, therefore, if you want to go more deeply into a subject you may do so, because you are not constrained by others who might wish to move on to something different.

Desmond Keegan (Kensington Park College, Adelaide, South Australia) cites the following disadvantages in his writings:

No heard language

This is only strictly true in the case of pure correspondence courses. Most distance learning courses that emanate from universities are linked with radio and television broadcasts and sometimes tapes, so some language is heard. Keegan cites the importance of this within the framework of interpersonal communication. He and many other educators feel that some students may feel the lack of it.

Absence of non-language communication

He is referring to what is discussed in Chapter 11 of this book, i.e. the way in which one learns by the use of other senses – sight, smell, touch etc. – and the way in which this improves memory and understanding.

Absence of feedback processes from student to teacher

This is debatable. There is rarely a total absence of feedback, even in poor-quality correspondence courses. Most well-structured distance learning courses allow for more than just correspondence; telephone calls and some face-to-face sessions are often built in.

Absence of feedback processes from teacher to student

Again, this is rarely true. But it is true that it is up to the student aggressively to seek interaction with the tutor. The amount of access to the tutor should always be determined before the start of the course.

Delayed reinforcement

This refers to the time delay involved between submitting an assignment and being told whether it is correct/good/well-structured etc. Those studying alone have to learn patience and maintain a high level of confidence to compensate for delays in communication.

Absence of student-to-student communication

This is the biggest drawback of studying alone. You do not have the opportunity to enter into group discussions, to develop your inter-personal skills and to learn from others, although there are ways round this, as we shall discuss later in this chapter. It is worth mentioning that for some people, lack of student-to-student communication is not necessarily a drawback. In the case of those with physical or social handicaps, the anxiety caused by trying to fit into a group may be too great and may cause their studies to suffer. Studying alone allows some people the possibility of real achievement without additional stress.

Lack of non-cognitive learning processes, e.g. peer support, peer criticism, peer contact etc.

What this means is that the solo student has to find other ways of learning these life skills: how to deal with people, how to overcome anxieties, how to support and be supported by others, how to treat criticism as a positive learning tool, and so on. However, this need not be a problem, as research has shown that the majority of students who choose to take up distance learning are older, have families and/or demanding jobs, and have therefore already acquired life skills.

The disadvantages, as recognised by the experts, can be overcome. First, you must analyse your own abilities to work alone. Secondly, you must recognise the drawbacks and consider how you will work to overcome them. Thirdly, you must choose your course very carefully.

Is it for you?

Working alone requires a special personality. You have to motivate, organise, discipline and criticise yourself; no one else can do it for you. You need to be ruthlessly honest with yourself if you are contemplating studying alone. Why do you want to pursue this course of study instead of studying with others? There are many bona fide reasons:

- You want a qualification, but you also have to work.

- You want a qualification but you need to stay at home raising small children.

- You want to do a particular course but the only one on offer is 200 miles away, so you have to do the correspondence alternative.

- You cannot leave home to study because you are looking after your elderly mother/father.

- You are physically disabled or ill and it is easier to study at home.

- You live in a remote part of the country and cannot easily get to an institute of education.

- You are a pensioner and would be embarrassed to attend a university at your time of life. (This is not really a valid reason for studying alone, but some people would view it as a major obstacle).

Apart from applying yourself to your studies, you also have to take care of your psychological needs. This means:

Banishing self-doubt

There will be times when you feel you are not doing very well in your studies because the feedback from your tutors is too impersonal and you have no classroom standard by which to measure yourself. You have to reassure yourself that if you were doing badly the tutors would tell you. If that still does not convince you, contact them with the specific request for them to be honest about your standard of work. Most tutors are only too pleased to respond to a student who genuinely wants to do better. Of course, self-doubt can creep in if you feel you are struggling with the course. The way to avoid this is to choose very carefully in the beginning.

Overcoming anxieties

We have already talked about this in Chapter 3. You have to work through your anxiety by, eventually, talking it through with someone. As you are working alone, it is a good idea to get a member of the family or a friend to take an interest in your studies before you start. You must have someone to talk to. Even if they do not understand the fine detail of your course, they have to care about you and your well-being. When you choose a course, also make sure that there is a student counsellor on the end of a phone available for distance learning students.

Getting things into perspective

Try to rationalise any fears you may have. Talking to others will help to put things into perspective. Most problems can be overcome, given time and help. Never panic about anything. Even money worries can be sorted out slowly. Citizens' Advice Bureaux will always help with practical problems. If you have a problem with your studies, perhaps it can be solved by a break from them. Discuss it with your tutor. After all, this is the freedom that Dave Stewart talked about; you do not have to work to a timetable; you can take as much time as you want. Most correspondence courses have the facility to suspend studies to allow you a period to get over money/work/family/health problems. It is your choice.

Strengthening your motivation

This is first and foremost your responsibility. You motivate yourself to study. Other factors may contribute. For example, if you are a single mother and you desperately want to make a better life for yourself and your children, every time they ask you for something you cannot afford it strengthens your will to succeed. However, you are the one who has to summon up reasons for carrying on and doing well. Your attitude to your studies is vital. Remember your objectives!

Students who study in groups are fortunate to have their motivation boosted by the atmosphere of competition, and by the support and encouragement of their peer group. You do not have that, but it certainly helps to have the support and encouragement of your nearest and dearest. Without that, studying can be very difficult.

Overcoming loneliness

Loneliness is made worse when you have nothing to occupy your brain. Your studies should keep loneliness at bay as long as you concentrate on them and enjoy them. At other times you can always reach out to others – go to independent lectures, form a letter or telephone partnership with another student, and so on.

Studying alone will not *make* you lonely. The chances are that you are lonely anyway because of other factors in your life. You cannot just do a job/look after your house and family, and study. You *must* have some social life. *Do not use a study programme to fill a void in your life that should be filled by human contact.* Shutting yourself away even more will not alleviate your loneliness.

Overcoming boredom

This is a problem for every student, but when you are on your own and do not have to face a tutor the next day and explain why you haven't tackled an assignment, it is all too easy to 'throw in the towel'. You have to be really tough. Promise yourself a really good reward when you have finished the boring stuff!

Coping with distractions at home

There are two problems here:

■ Other people at home do not respect your need for privacy and study time. Give them a stiff talking-to and get them to change their ways!

■ You allow yourself to be distracted too easily by being seduced away from your work to do some housework/make a cup of tea/watch television etc. If you cannot overcome your weak will you must remove yourself from home to study, if this is possible (i.e. if you do not have a very good reason for staying). Take yourself off to a library, for example. If you have no choice but to work at home, you must develop a resistance to your weak will! Plan a system of rewards, e.g. you work for two hours then you sit and watch television and have a cup of tea for an hour. Then you work for two more hours. You give yourself planned days off. Every Tuesday is your day for relaxing and not studying. Set yourself targets and rewards and you may find it easier. If it still does not work, you may have to face the fact that you are not cut out to study alone, and need to think of something else.

Which is the right course for you?

Choosing the right course is important for all students, but it is exceptionally important if you are to be studying alone, because it will cause you great anxiety later on if you have not chosen wisely.

Remember that the student who copes alone has to be, in many ways, superior in ability and knowledge to the student who is able to feed off a group. It is also more difficult to start from a position of total ignorance of a subject if you are a lone student, because you cannot ask questions and get instant answers. Your learning curve will be much longer than that of a student learning in a group. So it is unwise to undertake distance study in a subject of which you have no prior knowledge or experience, unless you are approaching it in stages. For example, you may eventually wish to take a degree in a particular subject, but it might be wise to take a GCSE or A level course first, if you have never studied that particular subject before.

When choosing your course remember that a good course should offer the following:

- A good presentation of study matter in easily-understood language with clear visuals and a lively format.

- Detailed advice to the student on how to approach the subject matter, extra reading matter, areas of research, pitfalls of certain subjects, advice on how to present material etc.

- An invitation to offer opinions and to analyse topics so that a productive two-way exchange can be built up between students and tutor.

- Contact by phone, or fax, if possible, with the tutor/s, principal and other members of staff, for urgent discussions. (This does not mean they should provide you with a 24 hour helpline, or that you should abuse a telephone privilege by using it constantly to discuss trivial matters.)

- Contact with other students. This demonstrates tutors' confidence in their course.

- The occasional face-to-face tutorial if possible, or a weekend seminar, a summer school etc.

- Back-up course material in the form of tapes, videos, television or radio broadcasts to allow for variety.

- A facility to allow easy termination or temporary suspension of the course in the case of a problem. This, of course, works from both sides. If the course is well run and the tutors genuinely care about standards, they should advise you if they feel that your capabilities are not sufficient to enable you to continue or complete the course.

- Recognised status of the course, so that its completion will be recognised and appreciated by other centres of learning or future employers.

- The course should be structured so it has realistic aims. There is no point in undertaking a course that expects such a high volume of work to be completed in such a short space of time that the average distance learning student could not achieve it.

When you are considering a particular course, ask to see as many examples as possible of the work involved and the schedules proposed. If you are considering a correspondence course which you hope will improve your employment prospects, check with major employers that the course has status. Make sure that the qualifications you hope to obtain will enable you to go on to further education should you wish.

Aim for objectivity

Read, listen to and analyse as much opinion on given subject matter as you can. Just because you are studying alone does not mean you do not have access to this. Read as many books on the subject and note the variations in opinion. Do not just stick to the recommended reading lists; subscribe to relevant journals or periodicals that will give you up-to-date opinions on relevant subjects. Keep a press cuttings file of any articles that appear that may add to your weight of opinion.

If time or circumstance allow, you could attend some independent lectures or seminars. There are lots of organisations who regularly hold meetings – chambers of commerce, libraries, art galleries, local societies and so on.

Ask your tutor if there is another student on the same course with whom you can correspond, or whom you may telephone, so the two of you can have wide-ranging discussions.

Objectivity is discussed more fully in Chapter 10.

And remember...

Whether you are studying alone or in a group, you need to organise yourself, manage your time, set targets, motivate yourself – and succeed. The lone student requires more self-discipline, but that is perhaps compensated for by a greater determination and a stronger motivation. Certainly, to know at the end of the day that you have achieved a goal all by yourself is extremely satisfying and equips you with one life skill which is of inestimable value – that of self-sufficiency.

Case histories

Case 4

The problem
Peter has severe epilepsy which, although controlled by drugs,

---

prevents him from driving a car. He wanted to take a degree but travel to and from the nearest university is impossible without a car.

The solution

He therefore elected to do an Open University degree. The courses are written by full-time course teams comprising OU staff and BBC staff. There is a total learning package comprising printed materials, television programmes, audio and video cassettes and anything else that is needed, such as home experiment kits for science courses.

A complex infrastructure supports the students. It consists of:

- An individual course tutor

- A personally assigned counsellor

- Regional study centres where students can gather occasionally to meet and use the resources

- Planned face-to-face tutorials throughout the year, if possible

- Home visits occasionally for the truly housebound

- Residential summer schools

- A student association with regional branches

- An on-going programme of strict assessment of students' and tutors' work so that problems can be highlighted and dealt with.

Therefore, although Peter does most of his studying alone, he can reach out for assistance and contact with other students whenever needed.

Case 5

The problem

Marian, who retired early and is in her fifties, felt that she would like to take two A levels as a serious hobby. She attends two local evening classes a week, but mostly works on her own. She has no contact with her tutors other than at the evening classes.

The solution

She has, however, become friendly with two other students, and they regularly exchange views over coffee or lunch. As one of her A levels is music, Marian often goes to lectures and seminars held at a local arts centre. She finds some of them helpful for her studies. The local music society also has occasional guest speakers.

Case 6

The problem

Wendy is a mother of two pre-school children, who take up all her time during the day. She decided to take a correspondence course in interior design and studies in the evenings and part of the weekend. The course is mostly correspondence, with some video tapes. There is a week-long summer school on offer, but she would find it almost impossible to leave her children for a whole week. She is able, occasionally, to have a day in London and attend seminars at RIBA (the Royal Institute of British Architects), the Victoria and Albert Museum or make other relevant trips. She is finding her course difficult because of the lack of interaction with other students.

The solution

She is contemplating stopping and resuming when the children start school. In the meantime, she hopes to continue her interest in design by attending a local evening class, once a week, in general art and design.

6 How to Study: try teamwork

There is great benefit in sharing the study process, because it enables you to draw on others' opinions, talents, resources and time. It should also help raise your own standards of study, not by leaning on others and letting them do the work, but by co-operating and learning the value of teamwork.

Several heads are better than one

Group discussions can be formal or informal. There may be no more than two or three of you having a conversation about your study subjects over a cup of coffee in the college canteen.

To take advantage of even this simple stage of discussion you need to overcome any shyness and reserve and engage in real conversation. Don't hang back and hope that others will come to you and start a conversation. If you loiter unobtrusively near a lively group of people, you may sometimes be able to gain the benefit of all their opinions without actually joining in yourself, but don't count on this as a method that will see you through your entire student life!

Group discussion has to be engineered most of the time, either by students or tutors. Some tutors find it a valuable process; they act as mediator, carefully directing the cut and thrust of the argument. There is also value, however, in students having discussions away from the guiding hand of the tutor. It comes back to the need to develop life skills. You need to develop your ability to weigh arguments, listen to the opinions of others and make your contribution rationally, without tempers being lost or relationships damaged. You can't always have a mediator present.

Why don't you initiate the idea of a discussion? Set the ball rolling and offer your home as a venue, with coffee thrown in. Others could perhaps be persuaded to act as host next time.

You could advertise on the college noticeboard for like-minded people to get together on college premises for a discussion. There must be a strict purpose to it, however. People are more likely to turn up if you state your objectives, e.g. 'Want to discuss the latest theories in physics with like-minded people? Ring 01993 7271 and we'll get together'.

Group discussion enables students to listen, learn, disagree, put forward opinions and rationalise arguments, but there is also another purpose – to learn to be part of a team. A group discussion may not seem like teamwork but any interaction between a group of people is part of what teamwork is all about. During group discussion you will find that natural leaders emerge – not necessarily those who have the loudest opinions, but those who keep drawing the argument back to its original point, reminding people that they have already spoken or already stated that argument, or that they should allow someone else to speak.

Note-taking is an important part of group discussions. Not, perhaps, during a hurried chat in the canteen, but in a more structured discussion or a formal debate.

Two's company

Studying as a twosome is something that often starts when we are small children at school. It is born out of friendship and a genuine desire to help each other. Later in life it can have the same basis, or be a more business-like arrangement in which you form an alliance with a like-minded person with similar abilities in order to study. You may not be close friends or socialise together.

Studying with someone who has similar abilities to you, but a different perspective, can give an added dimension to your work. There are several things you need to guard against, however:

- *You must preserve your individuality*
  You must be aware of your different styles and call the experiment to a halt if one of you starts sounding or writing like the other.

- *You both have to pull your weight*
  The experiment has gone wrong if one of you starts relying on the other for continual assistance.

- *You have to share resources*
  This means, unless it is mutually inconvenient, splitting the burden of where, when and how you study. Your place this week, his place next week, and so on.

- *You must not write your papers together*
  You can share notes, research and opinions, but you must work individually when the time comes to write papers. No tutor will accept identical papers from two students, even if you each vary the odd paragraph.

- *You must have periods of studying alone*
  Guard your self-reliance. Even in marriage, you cannot expect to be continually supported in all your efforts in life. It is advisable not to get too used to constant support now.

Lending a helping hand

If you are a bright student you may be asked to help someone who is having difficulties – perhaps they are disabled, have missed some lectures, or are studying in a second language. Don't turn down the request unless there are very good reasons why you cannot help, because the opportunity to pass knowledge on to someone else can be valuable to you as well as them. By dealing with someone else's questions you will increase your own knowledge of the subject, and, by breaking down your level of knowledge and communicating it to someone at a lower level of knowledge, you will acquire an important skill. It will help you to become a good communicator.

However, make sure the arrangement it time-limited. You can't afford to devote too much of your own valuable study time to helping someone else. Such an arrangement should be for a limited period only and should benefit you both. The person you are helping should acquire a level of self-reliance and then be encouraged to get on with it.

If you initiate such an arrangement out of pity for someone it could backfire on you. They may not realise they need help, may resent your interference or cling to you so you find it difficult to free yourself. Such an arrangement should be set up by a third party, and only where the disadvantaged student has asked for help and all parties have agreed on a time limit.

Shared study

This is a very popular approach in the USA. Several students, perhaps as many as six, choose to share the burden of gathering together material for essays, projects and other assignments. When it works well it is very effective and brings the benefit of continuous interaction with other students. However, before considering setting up a shared study group, the following points should be remembered:

- Everyone should have the same level of capabilities

- Everyone must have the same aims

- Everyone must derive the same benefits from the exercise

- Everyone must share tasks equally

- Everyone must agree to establish rules and methods of work.

Capabilities

This doesn't mean you should make your study group exclusive. No study group should be based on whether or not a student's 'face fits', but only on whether a student is on the same level, academically, as the rest of the group. You must analyse your own position before agreeing to band together with other individuals. Be honest with yourself. If you are far ahead of the others for whatever reason, you will not fit in, and this will only cause resentment amongst the others. On the other hand, if you are lagging behind you cannot, in all fairness, latch on to a group in the hope that they will pull you up. A shared study group works best when everyone starts from the same point and hopes to finish at the same point.

Aims

Everyone must have the same goal – to achieve a level of quality in their studies – and the same level of commitment. Entering into a shared study programme means agreeing to be part of a team and agreeing to work hard as an individual for the benefit of the group. If you are seeking to join an established group, you must decide whether you can give the amount of time and effort the group requires. You may have to work as well as study, and so may not be able to attend regular group meetings or get to libraries during normal opening hours to do the necessary research that would be part of your contribution. However, the group may have built into its operation the varying time availabilities of its members. It may be able to accommodate you and give you a workload which is within your capabilities.

Benefits

Everyone must derive the same benefits from shared study. That is to say you must get what you need from the experience, otherwise it is not for you. If your primary need is to be able to discuss each assignment with others and get valuable feedback and opinions, but the rest of the group do not want to have a discussion, preferring instead to concentrate on gathering the research material, you are not getting what you need from the group. A shared study group should decide, at the outset, what its aims and methods will be, and ensure that all members are catered for.

Sharing tasks

It is important that everyone shares the workload equally and shares information fully with the other members. It is also important that discussion time is shared equally; everyone should get a say.

Rules and methods

This is the important part. You have to have rules and you have to have a leader – but you also have to be democratic. In a democracy, a leader is one who is chosen by the others, not one who merely assumes the position because of natural dominance. The best study groups view the exercise as a valuable teamwork/life skills experience and give everyone the chance of being leader in turn, say, for a three-month period.

The group has to decide at the outset what its function is, what its aims are and how it will operate. This is the point at which you decide whether or not it is for you. If you cannot match the level of commitment of the others, or you feel uneasy about being bound by the rules, pull out.

The good news

Working in a study group can develop the following skills:

Forming relationships

It is possible to go through a course of study and bury yourself in your books without developing interpersonal skills. This will not be of benefit in the real world. Even the most high-minded research scientists have to deal with people when they leave university and find a job.

Working in a team

Being part of a team is hard, particularly if you are a dominant individual who likes to be alone, centre stage. However, it's good discipline to learn to bow to the will of the majority and to work in an environment where everyone has an equal say and an equal input. Similarly, those who are shy and retiring should find, in a team that works well, that they are drawn out of their shell and contribute more.

Solving problems

Several people can always solve problems better than one person working alone. A different perspective from another person is valuable, as is a mixture of negative and positive personalities. You may be a person for whom the glass is always half-empty, but put you with a person for whom the glass is always half-full and a balance is achieved. It is often very stimulating to be involved in a group problem-solving session because you begin to realise how different individuals approach problems in different ways. Thus you enhance your own ability to weigh up all the possibilities and solve problems on your own.

Being creative

Some people seem to be full of ideas very early on; others are led by the encouragement and example of others. The experience of working in a team, where creativity is fed by the discussion process, can help you develop a creative turn of mind. It has been said that there are no new ideas, only recycled old ones. If this is true, you need plenty of experience of listening to other people's ideas so you can recycle them later on!

Persuasiveness

Bringing a group round to your way of thinking is achieved by persuasiveness, not by bullying, sulking or shouting. Developing the ability to be persuasive only comes with practice. It comes with an understanding of the motivations of individuals, so you get to know which buttons to press to elicit a response.

Decision making

Learning to make decisions as a group may be hard if you have always been used to making your own decisions, but it will give you the opportunity to develop the ability to play the devil's advocate with yourself later in life, and to make decisions based on sound reason, not just instinct.

Information gathering

The way in which we gather information is often very personal. You can learn from others' methods and teach them yours. This can be valuable.

Presentation of information

The value of group work is that you have to present information twice – first to the group and then, jointly, to others outside the group. This helps you refine your presentation techniques. The final presentation, of course, has the benefit of the group's input and should be far superior to anything you could have done alone.

Learning from your peers

This is the most important lesson in life. It is easy to learn from superiors and acknowledged experts, but if you can learn to open your mind and learn from your equals, you will be the richer.

Influencing decisions

This comes down to persuasiveness again, but it also includes learning how to present material in a manner likely to influence a group decision. You have to learn how to present material to maximum effect – the right time to present it and the manner in which to present it. Making people listen to you, without raising your voice, is a quality worth developing.

Networking

This over-used word simply means making your talents and abilities known to others and getting to know their talents and abilities so that, at some point in the future, you can be of mutual benefit to each other. It should not mean using people for your own gain. The idea is that you support each other: like for like, benefit for benefit. Working as a team, making friends amongst students who are not on the same course, joining societies and clubs are all ways of establishing an infrastructure of contacts for the time when you have finished your studies.

Target setting

This is an essential part of teamwork and of studying. First you have to identify your targets and then you have to discuss, solve problems, make decisions and work to achieve those targets.

Coping with change

Changes in course, tutors or students can all be better coped with as a group because you are there to support each other whenever necessary.

Managing other people

Someone has to be leader of the group and manage the others. This has responsibilities as well as pleasures. The person who is leader for that appointed time has to control the meetings, encourage the quiet members, tone down the loud ones, take the lazy ones to task and praise the hard workers. He or she has to set the agenda, allocate the jobs and review the results.

Of course, it is not just the leader of the group who has to learn to manage people. Everyone has to, albeit in a subtler way. Managing people is about understanding people – their talents, their limits, their motivations. Getting people to perform to the best of their ability is about support, encouragement and acknowledgement. Curb your desire to belittle others, to pressurise them or to ignore their work. This is not a productive attitude and will only speed your exit from a team.

Moving groups

Even though you may be part of a shared study group, a situation may arise where a tutor puts you, for the purpose of tackling a particular assignment, temporarily in a group that is not of your creation.

This group may be made up of people of mixed abilities, either deliberately or unconsciously, and it may provide many challenges. You may find yourself grouped together with a mixed bag of people – the good, the bad, the lazy, the indifferent. Even if you have initial feelings of despair, you should be able to use the skills you have gained in your own study group to good effect in this new situation. Do your new group a favour and quickly teach them how to work as a team. Give them a chance to try and work as a cohesive group. It could be the best test of 'people management' you have ever had!

Of course, if the experiment goes on for any length of time, you will have to try and balance your commitments to both groups. This could be tricky. Put organisational skills into overdrive and plan a new schedule of work.

The bad news

Shared study sounds ideal, but it can be fraught with difficulties. We are talking about personalities here. Sometimes it is impossible to merge certain personalities into a team and you have to recognise failure when it arises. If one group does not work, don't abandon the concept entirely. Give yourself a rest for a while and concentrate on your solo studies. You can perhaps try to form another group with different individuals later on. Your studies and their successful completion are what is important. Remember your initial objectives! If a study group spends more time arguing than actually doing the work, it has failed. Don't waste time trying to revive it. Move on.

7   Notes, Notes, Notes

Do you need to take notes? Absolutely. Even if you have a photo-graphic or a highly retentive memory, you should always make the effort to have a permanent record of everything you have listened to, read or viewed. Effective note-taking is a very important skill. It is the basis of your studies.

It is therefore very important that you take notes in the way that is of most use to you. If you can't read your notes when you come to use them, or the information that you have noted down is of little use, you have wasted your time.

If you are returning to education after a lengthy time away from study you will need to learn (or re-hone) these skills.

Work out a system of note-taking that works for you, based on the principles in this chapter; there is no more important skill to be acquired at the start of a higher education course. Remember, your object is to succeed; effective note-taking is one of the cornerstones of your future success.

Why take notes?

Taking notes has a five-fold purpose:

- It helps you to concentrate on the subject matter in hand.

- It helps to improve your memory.

- It highlights gaps in information and stimulates questions.

- It should stimulate you to research further on a topic.

- The logical analysis of notes is the first step in presenting more detailed information in an essay, thesis, project or presentation.

Notes help you concentrate

If you are just listening to a lecture or radio programme without taking notes, it effectively leaves a part of your brain free to wander off at the slightest distraction or degree of boredom. The act of taking notes whilst listening requires a greater effort from the brain and therefore makes you concentrate on the information being given.

Notes are a memory aid

This topic is covered in greater detail in Chapter 11. Memory is made up of all the senses – hearing, sight, smell, touch and so on. The more senses you use in establishing a record of a particular subject, action, person or activity, the greater will be your powers of recall. Therefore, if you write something down at the same time as you are listening to it or reading it, you are using more than one sense and thus giving yourself more than one chance of remembering.

People's memories work in different ways. You may be a person who remembers visually rather than by hearing ('I'm terrible at names but I always remember faces'). When you try to remember a subject, what flashes through your mind is the visual image of the words on the page.

Notes stimulate

Notes should not just be a precise record of what you are hearing; they should also remind you of:

- something you have just heard that you do not understand and which requires clarification

- a subject, touched on briefly, that you want to follow up in more detail

- something you have just heard that you dispute and wish to argue with

- something you didn't hear very well or missed that you need to have repeated.

Note-taking is not a passive exercise, but an active exercise in intellectual stimulation; notes are aids to understanding and analysing.

The active note-taker should also be stimulated to take the questions/disputes/gaps in their knowledge evidenced by their notes and use them as aids for further study.

Notes are the first step in an essay

Notes are, of course, the first step in the preparation of a more lengthy written work. If you do not take notes initially, you will have to create them at a later date when you come to map out your detailed written work. The most effective way to approach assignments is first to make a sequential plan of information, using keywords and sub-headings as memory triggers. This is covered more fully in Chapter 10.

Take notes which work for you

Everyone writes notes in their own way. Usually only you have to understand them and that is all that matters. Some people can take down a whole lecture verbatim because they can do shorthand. However advantageous this may seem, it does have one drawback. Fast shorthand writers are like fast copy typists who do not necessarily read what they are typing, the mind just locks on to translating words into shorthand and sometimes the meaning is lost. Therefore the opportunities to analyse, question or dispute what is being heard are also lost. It is only later, when transcribing the shorthand into written English, that the sense of what has been said comes into focus.

Most people do adopt one of two methods when note-taking – linear or 'tree'. A linear approach is simply making notes line after line on a page, using keywords, abbreviated words or half sentences in order to keep up with the speech (see Figure 1, page 61).

'Tree' note-taking is where people make keywords or headings into a kind of tree which represents to them the logical flow of information (see Figure 2, page 62).

However you take your notes, it is helpful to remember the following points:

- time
- space

- comprehension
- order
- legibility
- revision
- achievement.

Time

Allow yourself time to breathe between taking notes, which means learning to make minimal notes with maximum information content. You cannot rush along at breakneck speed trying to take notes at the same pace as they are being spoken. You need to distinguish the important words and phrases which distil the essence of the subject matter.

Space

Give yourself space in your notes to add information, underline, query, ask questions and make notes within notes. If you are note-taking by the linear system, double space your lines and allow yourself wide margins. It may be that the person giving the lecture or making the broadcast, or the author of the book you are reading does not present their information in a logical sequence and, as their subject matter flits backwards and forwards, you may have to amend your notes accordingly.

Comprehension

The point of taking notes is that they reflect your understanding of subject matter and provide you with accurate material on which to base further study. If you do not understand something and the lecturer cannot solve the problem, or you are taking notes from a broadcast or a book where there is no one to immediately answer your query, make a note so you can research the answers later on. Ifyou find that you do not understand some of your own keywords or ciphers, cross-check with others taking the same notes. Ask them while their memories are fresh – do not leave it until later.

Fig 1

Handwritten notes in linear form

Registering a death

Following people, in precedence, must register death.
Failure - fine of £50.

1/ Relative present at death
2/ Relative - there during illness (not death)
3/ Rel. - living in registr area
4/ Anyone present at death
5/ Anyone living in house where d. occurred
6/ Person respons. for burial or crem.

} if death happens in house or hospital

If death happens elsewhere
1/ Any relative of dead person
2/ Anyone present at death
3/ Any. who found body
4/ As no 6 above

Fig 2

Handwritten notes in 'tree' form

Registering a death

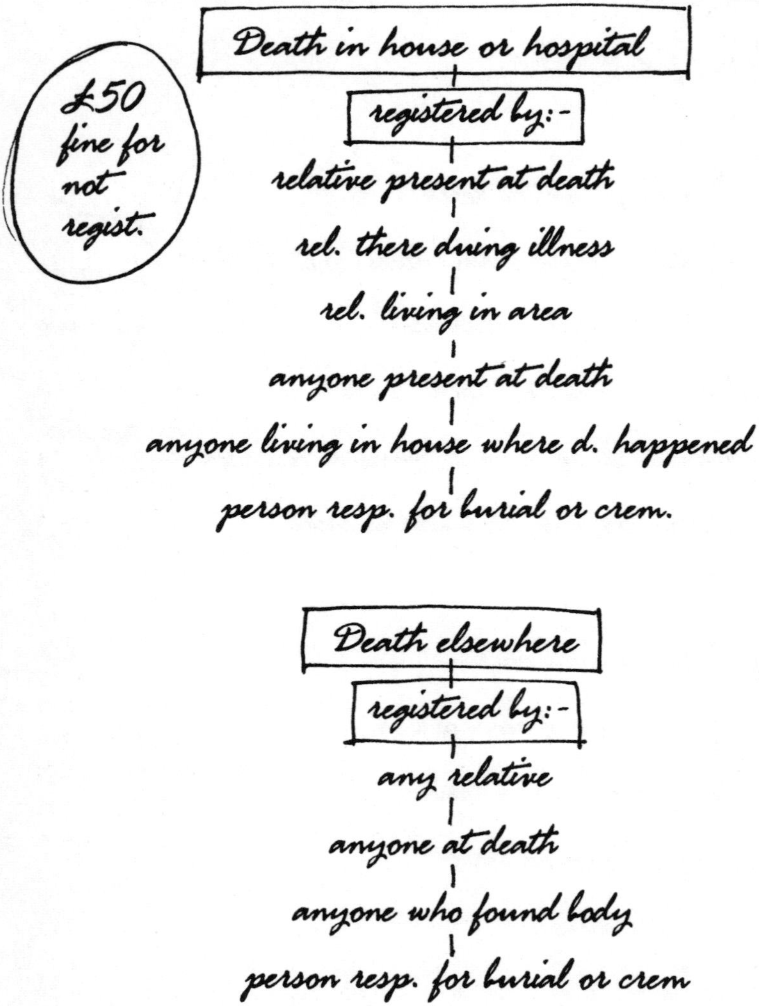

Death in house or hospital

registered by:-

relative present at death

rel. there during illness

rel. living in area

anyone present at death

anyone living in house where d. happened

person resp. for burial or crem.

£50 fine for not regist.

Death elsewhere

registered by:-

any relative

anyone at death

anyone who found body

person resp. for burial or crem

Similarly, if you missed something and there is a gap in your notes, ask the lecturer or fellow students while the topic is still current.

Order

The order of your notes should reflect a logical sequence of information. The fact that they do not may not be your fault. It may be that the information was presented in a haphazard way.

It is a good idea to summarise the main points of a lecture at the end of your notes, even if the lecturer does not do it. If the sequence of information was muddled or your notes are a jumble of additions or deletions, a summary will help you untangle your notes, when you come to revision.

Legibility

It may seem obvious to say that your notes should be readable, even if only by you. If they are barely readable at the time you take them, you may find them almost impossible to read weeks or months hence. There could also be an instance when you have left your notes at your digs, for example, gone home to visit mum and someone has to read them over the phone to you. If you struggle to decipher them, how will your flatmate cope?! A medical student I know assures me that doctors only develop bad handwriting after they leave medical school, otherwise none of them would ever get degrees!

Revision

It is a good idea to revise and edit notes as soon as possible after you have taken them. You can tidy them up, change the order, add in answered queries and tack on any bits of extra research you have done. You may also wish to transfer them on to your computer. Do whatever is of most use to you and your way of working. It is also another valuable exercise in memory recall and further preparation for essays. It is also a good idea to re-read the notes after a couple of weeks to make sure you still understand them.

Achievement

Your notes should achieve what you need them to achieve. They should be an accurate record of what you have heard, read or seen, they should stimulate your memory to recall greater detail of the subject, they should present a logical flow of information on which you can base a more detailed piece of written work, and they should stimulate you to analyse and research a topic further.

Lectures – some good, some bad

Problems in lectures can vary from the physical problems of not being able to hear or see very well, to there being too many people in the lecture room and not enough space to spread your books out, to you (or the lecturer) arriving late, or the lecturer being a poor or inadequate communicator.

The physical problems can be largely overcome by always arriving at lectures early so you can get a good seat and stake your claim for space in which to write.

Communication problems are difficult. A lecturer's speed of delivery may be too fast (you can't keep up) or too slow (you fall asleep); the information may be presented illogically (just when you think the lecturer has left something out, they bring the subject up and you get confused); the lecturer's train of thought may be easily distracted (and mischievous students know that every time they interrupt with a question the lecturer will go off at a tangent); your questions may not be answered satisfactorily (the lecturer may not fully understand them or you may have gone beyond the scope of the subject they are prepared to tackle); there may be too many irrelevances in the lecture (you came along expecting to hear hard facts and all you get are theories); or there are too many visuals and not enough words (the trouble with doing a business degree is that you get pie graphs and flow charts coming out of your ears).

All you can do is ask the lecturer if they can recommend further reading on the subject that has just been presented. You can go straight to the library and make your notes from source rather than relying on the patchy notes you took during the lecture.

Taking notes from broadcasts and programmes

Here you have an advantage because you can tape radio broadcasts and video television programmes, and many radio and television companies offer complete transcripts of the programme by post for a modest fee. This gives you the chance to devote your full attention to the broadcast or programme and have several attempts at making a good set of notes.

This is, perhaps, most important with television programmes, where the need to concentrate on the visual content is paramount and leaves you little time to make notes. With radio programmes, you should have enough time during the programme to make notes. Making a tape recording (perhaps for use later when revising) can be useful since there may be a delay before you get your transcript through the post, so it is best not to rely on this as a primary source of information.

The disadvantage of broadcasts and programmes is that you can't ask questions. If you have the time, it may be possible to track down the programme producer/presenter and put your questions in a letter, but it is more likely you will have to find your answers elsewhere.

Taking notes from books

Even if you own textbooks, do not write in them. Some people scribble comments and queries all over books, which defaces them. It is also foolish, since course textbooks in good condition can be sold to other students when they have ceased to be of interest to you. Library books, of course, should never be defaced. Nothing infuriates book lovers more than to find that someone has written facetious comments in the margins. Write notes, comments, questions and answers in notebooks. Let others draw their conclusions from the published texts alone.

The art of précis, which you may have thought was a useless subject at school, comes into its own here. It is not just the art of condensing a whole page or more of written material into one neat paragraph; it is also the discipline that teaches you critically to appraise information in order to extract what is important and discard what is irrelevant.

Remember that authors are not always disciplined in their presentation of information, nor are publishers always blessed with good editors who can whip any amount of waffle into shape. If you make notes as you read each page, you may find yourself getting into a muddle if the author has decided to depart from the straight and narrow. It is best to read each chapter in full, making a précis of each. That way you get a better overall picture of what is important and what is irrelevant.

Underneath the précis you can list important details such as names, places, dates, formulae, calculations, further reading, quotations etc. (see Figure 3 over).

Taking notes from magazines, newspapers, journals and reports

The same can be said for articles in these media. Read the whole, then précis and list crucial pieces of information.

Remember...

If you can strive for an orderly mind at the outset of your studies, i.e. the note-taking stage, then the more demanding aspects of your study programme, when you have to communicate back to your educators what you have learnt, should follow more easily. A good set of well-constructed notes that are easily understandable and perform all the functions we have discussed are the foundation stone on which you will build solid learning structures.

Fig 3: Précis and notes

Précis of Chapter 7 of 'The Countryside Manual'
by Stephenson, Manderby Press

The author discusses in this chapter how the various changes in the weather show themselves in the living things which depend so much upon them.

He mentions all the country sayings about weather portents (some listed below).

Most responsive to weather changes are the plants. A flag of seaweed hung on the wall will turn harsh and dry in fine weather, becoming moist and soft and pliable when rain is imminent. Flowers that close their petals when rain is near are the scarlet pimpernel, the daisy and the chickweed amongst others. Animals are also sensitive. Many creatures show unusual activity before storms. Rooks are a good guide to weather conditions: if they fly low, it means rain, if they feed busily and hurry about together, a storm is likely, if they sit about on fences or dart down and wheel about, it means wind. Before a storm seagulls fly inland. He cites other examples of animal activity (see below). Some scientists used living creatures in weather experiments (see below).

Notes

Sayings:

'Seagull, seagull, sit on the sand
It's never fine weather when you're inland.'

'Oak before ash, all wet and splash.'
'Ash before oak, all fire and smoke' (refers to blossom and whether summer will be wet or dry).

ANIMAL ACTIVITY BEFORE RAIN

Cats - wash behind ears

Spiders - come out of webs

Crickets - chirp

Fish - rise to top of pond

Flies & gnats - more active

Frogs - croak

EXPERIMENT

Mr Merryweather drew up a chart, which he presented at the Royal Exhibition of 1851, which showed the activity of leeches during all kinds of weather. He offered his leech storm glass to the Admiralty for use in lighthouses.

8   Effective Research

The quality of your research says much about how enquiring your mind is, how inventive and creative you are, how resourceful and how determined. It is simplicity itself to find the books you are told to find and to travel no further than your campus library or local library. How unimaginative! We have a society which is devoted to communicating, to recording, to storing and to creating information. How sad not to at least dip into that great wealth, even if it does take a little bit of effort.

All the skills you develop during a study programme should be of use elsewhere in life, and the art of researching is the most useful. We live in a society that collects information, but society is largely bureaucratic and so does not believe in wasting too much effort disseminating that information. You have to go and look for it.

How to go about it

Research doesn't have to take place in libraries, although they are likely to be the starting place. Sources of information also include commerce and industry, the Internet, databases and CD-ROMs.

Good research can involve:

- reading relevant literature
- correspondence with people and organisations
- conversations with people and organisations
- observation of work in progress, other people's research
- hands-on experience of work practices, technology, crafts etc.
- visiting places of interest – museums, countries

- experiments
- group discussions
- group efforts.

Group discussion and group efforts are usually part of a shared study scheme, which we looked at in Chapter 6.

Libraries: they don't just lend books

Let's pause here and say a swift prayer of thanks for the library system. Until you have lived in a country that does not have one you do not realise how privileged we are to have one of the most highly developed library systems in the world.

UK and worldwide access

Libraries are so much more than places that lend books. Any computerised library can access information from anywhere in the world. There are a very large number of databases. For example, press databases can give the user a full text or précis of articles and news items appearing in British and foreign newspapers. Even uncomputerised libraries can order books from anywhere in the world via the British Library system. It just takes a little time and patience. Most large reference libraries keep back issues of national newspapers such as *The Times* on microfiche. These are fully indexed, so a researcher can, for example, look up all the articles that have appeared on pig farming in the last two years, read the relevant microfiches on the special machine and copy the articles, all within the space of half an hour.

The computer networks of most libraries usually extend throughout a county, so if you want a particular book or copy of a journal which does not appear to be in your library, the librarian should be able to find out, via the computer, which library within the county holds the publication that you want, and, in the case of a lending book, whether or not it is out on loan.

A copy of every book

Since 1709, when the first Copyright Act was passed, certain libraries in the UK have received one free copy of every book ever published in the UK. These libraries are:

The Bodleian Library in Oxford
The Cambridge University Library
The National Library of Scotland in Edinburgh
Trinity College Library, Dublin
The National Library of Wales in Aberystwyth
The British Library in London.

It is possible to go to these libraries and apply for a researcher's ticket, which costs nothing and is valid for one or more years. This allows the researcher to request any of the books in the archive. Not all the books are stored on site, of course, so requests may not be granted that day. Even books that are stored on site may be in use by others, so a wait is involved.

University and private libraries

There are many university and private libraries which are not open to the general public but which usually open to bona fide researchers/students. A directory which lists all the libraries and the subject of their collections is published by AsLib.

There are also many unusual locations for libraries. Some of the larger foreign embassies, for example, have libraries and can assist in obtaining special material – the US Embassy in London is a case in point. Large manufacturing or commercial organisations have libraries, as do teaching hospitals, trade union offices and so on.

Directories

Libraries also have directories, such as *Whitaker's* or the *English Catalogue* which will enable a researcher to trace a book when they only know the title or just the author or even just the subject matter. Most libraries also have on microfiche details of which books are still in print. If they are out of print you are back to accessing them through one of the archive libraries mentioned above or using an antiquarian bookseller (at a fee) to find the book for you.

'Books in Progress'

For students who are themselves toying with the idea of eventually publishing a book and think they have found a topic as yet untouched, there is a 'Books in Progress' register operated by the National Book League. It is not comprehensive by any means, since the writers give the information voluntarily, but you should be able to find out if your 'undiscovered' topic has already been discovered by someone else who is about to rush into print with it. It is also a useful means of finding out who may have fresh information on a topic you are researching. If you write to the author of the book in progress they may be persuaded to answer some questions.

Newspapers – national and international

Most libraries hold, at most, ten years of back issues of the standard national and international newspapers. Further back than that and you have to go to the British Library Newspaper Library in Colindale, London. This library also stocks periodicals, although scientific and technical periodicals are housed at The British Library Science Reference Library in Holborn and Bayswater in London. Other subjects can be found at various libraries throughout the UK and, again, the AsLib directory of libraries will give the full information.

Official publications

Official publications, Government Papers, Acts of Parliament and so on are available in some measure from local reference libraries. Her Majesty's Stationery Office (HMSO) in Holborn, London, carries a full list of what can be obtained. There is an Official Publications Room at the British Library which houses both national and foreign official papers that go back quite a long way. However, any documents that may be classed as historical will be in the Public Records Office (PRO) in Kew and some are in their building in London. The PRO records go back to the eleventh century. HMSO publishes a list of what, in general terms, is available.

Filmed and recorded material

Filmed and recorded material is also of importance to student researchers. Filmed material is kept at the National Film Archive in London. The BBC Sound Archives are not open to the public, but staff may be able to answer queries.

A man (or woman) who knows

One could fill a whole book with the details of what is available through the library and archive systems. They are a veritable Aladdin's cave for the researcher. Anyone who thinks librarians just stamp dates in books should think again. Your reference librarian could open up a world of knowledge for you; all you have to do is ask.

Subjects at a glance: the Dewey system

All public libraries and most academic libraries arrange their books according to the Dewey Decimal system, which was invented by Mr Dewey, an American, in 1873. It is very simple, and keeping a small card with the classifications on it in your pocket will save you valuable time when you visit the library.

The Dewey system of numbers covers ten major subject areas:

General subjects (odds and ends)	000–099
Philosophy	100–199
Religion	200–299
Social Sciences	300–399
Language	400–499
Sciences	500–599
Technology	600–699
Art and Recreation	700–799
Literature	800–899
Geography, Biography and History	900–999

You may find that categories within categories have sprung up because certain subjects were not in demand in Mr Dewey's day. Business books, for example, will be found under Technology in the 600 number range. You may want to expand your pocket list to include a more detailed description of the categories.

Use indexes and footnotes: tap others' research

When researching published material, don't forget the value of using indexes and footnotes correctly. They are the fruits of someone else's research and can add greatly to yours.

Indexes, if done well, can highlight specific topics within a book and save you having to wade through the whole book. For example:

Second World War:
> causes of...   pp 22-36
> declaration of ... pp 36-38
> outbreak of ...   pp 38-47

If you are only interested in the *causes* of the Second World War you need only concern yourself with pages 22 to 36.

Most non-fiction books have a good index that is of great value to the researcher; it is a source of irritation that biographies are not so uniformly well equipped. Biographies often contain snippets of valuable material which is often difficult to extract quickly. For example, if you were trying to research the life and times of Noel Coward, you would find him cropping up in all sorts of theatrical and film autobiographies, but you would probably have to read most of them all the way through to extract the material you need.

Footnotes or endnotes should be the source of more detailed information. Footnotes are found at the bottom of pages bearing a number corresponding to one in the text. Endnotes are also numbered, but are found at the end of the chapter or the end of the book. Conscientious authors of non-fiction will usually tell you in footnotes and endnotes where they found an interesting quote or statistic. You can then get hold of that publication, paper or document and see if it holds further relevant information.

Contact commerce and industry: a source of information

Much research material emanates from commerce and industry. Firstly, there are the very expensive market reports generated on a regular basis by independent researchers: good business libraries should have reference copies of them. Some of these reports are comprehensive and show the past and current performance and future trends of particular sectors of industry.

Many organisations, for example, the large accountancy firms, operate like American universities by requiring all their senior partners to publish something during their careers. These pieces of research and advice are used to keep the firm's name to the fore and to establish it as a centre of excellence.

The Institute of Directors has a highly-rated library which provides access to domestic and foreign business information, as does the CBI and the British Institute of Management. Most of the trade associations such as the Advertising Association and the Market Research Society also offer library facilities.

Individual companies can be a good source of material, particularly if they conduct their own scientific, technological or market research. Many food retail chains, for example, have teams of dieticians, home economists and food scientists who research and write about the nutritional value of food, how to cook it, how to store it and so on. Companies that manufacture pharmaceuticals or household products are constantly carrying out medical and scientific research, which they eventually publish. Contact the public relations or customer services departments of these organisations to see whether they can help you.

Face-to-face research

Not all research can be done via the printed or the computerised word. Sometimes you have to talk to people to find things out. Here is an example from my own experience and from two other research projects.

Case history 7

During my years of study I was given the following assignment: 'Select a British industry and show its evolution during the post-war years and its status today'. Being something of a show-off and having reached a point in my studies where I needed to inject a little light relief into my work programme, I decided to choose something unusual. Off the top of my head I chose the British Christmas tree industry, not really knowing whether there was such a thing.

My first stop was the library, of course, and a publication which over the years has proved of inestimable value, *The Directory of British Associations*. One thing you can always rely on with the British is that if more than two of them are interested in the same thing, they form an association. Sure enough, there was an Association of Christmas Tree Growers and an Association of Christmas Tree Importers. Armed with this information I telephoned the relevant secretaries and had lengthy chats. I found out quite a lot about what was a billion pound industry. There were two sides to the industry – real trees and artificial trees. The two associations sent me annual reports and copies of their newsletters containing details of the industry's growth. I found out the name and phone number of a Christmas tree grower and an artificial tree manufacturer. I spoke to them. Then I spoke to several large retailers who stocked either real or artificial Christmas trees. Somewhere along the line I got involved with the Forestry Commission which has its own Christmas tree plantations and which also advises others. I collected more literature and sales catalogues.

By the time I came to present my report, it had burgeoned into several pages about an interesting, highly competitive and lucrative seasonal industry, prey to the vagaries of the weather, changes in Christmas fashion (remember the fad for all-white or -silver Christmas trees?), and not without its own scientific breakthroughs (genetically-engineered trees that do not shed needles, and ever more realistic fake trees).

The research was fun and certainly livened up my life.

Case history 8

Martin had to do a project on technology in offices during the 1940s. He knew a little about the subject from lectures. He knew that the facsimile machine or 'the wire' was used, in a primitive form, by newspaper offices during that period, and that adding machines were used, but that computers were still being invented and would come out of scientific breakthroughs made during the war.

When he came to do research in the libraries there was little or nothing that had been published. He went to the Science Museum

---

in London and there was able to discover a lot by actually seeing the adding machines, duplicating machines, typewriters and so on that were in use in the 1940s. There was still very little literature on the subject, however.

In desperation he phoned the Public Records Office to see if they could suggest anything. After some thought, they mentioned that they held a consultant's report from 1943, which detailed, criticised and made recommendations about the office practices and purchasing procedures of a Whitehall department. When Martin sat down in the Public Records Office and read this lengthy report, which contained photographs, it gave him most of what he needed. It detailed all the office machines currently in use; where the consultant considered they were outmoded, up-to-date replacements were suggested and descriptions given of their improved functions. Martin was allowed to photocopy the full report as a base for his project.

He then wrote to the government department in question to ask if any of their pensioners had been working in the department during the 1940s and would be prepared to talk to him about their office practices. The department contacted some and they in turn contacted Martin, amused to talk about such mundane matters. From them he uncovered such little gems as the fact that patriotic feeling ran so high during the war that most of the staff objected to using the office machinery, most of which was of German manufacture. It was this feeling in the marketplace which prompted American companies to copy a lot of German machines and cash in on the office technology market. 3M and IBM were born.

Case history 9

Danielle had chosen for her thesis the subject 'The Changing Population of the East End of London'. Of course, there was a great deal of published material detailing the history of the East End and the cultural changes it had undergone as the various ethnic groups moved in and out of the area. By far the most valuable piece of research that came her way, however, was when the borough of Tower Hamlets, attempting to refurbish a row of derelict terrace houses in Brick Lane, unwittingly uncovered a house which was a time capsule. The upstairs was an almost perfectly preserved Huguenot silk weaver's work place (a huge pane of glass had been installed in the roof to give the weaver maximum light by which to work), and the downstairs was an equally perfectly preserved miniature Jewish synagogue. Tower Hamlets handed it over to a group of archaeologists and Danielle was able to work with them and compile a breathtaking amount of research on the lives of these two separate East End communities, the Huguenots and the Eastern European Jewish émigrés, who had lived in the house 100 years apart. Details of everyday life were found under the floorboards and in cupboards: weavers' bobbins, pieces of clothing, toys, religious texts. In the backyard there was even a mulberry tree for the silkworms to feed on.

The months of observation and discussions with archaeologists were worth more than a hundred books.

Surfing the Internet

Over 30 million computers around the world can now connect to the Internet and it is estimated that this figure will reach around 200 million in less than five years time. At present, accessing the Internet requires a computer and modem. The majority of Internet users just use it to send and receive e-mail, but a significant minority of students and researchers 'surf the Net' in search of data they can use. The Internet, whose main language is English, has a variety of uses, such as access to downloadable computer files, which can be text, data, images or programmes. Another facility is a bulletin board which allows people from all over the world to join – or start – a 'discussion' on any topic. Perhaps the most useful facility for the researcher, however, is published information access. For example, UK Budget information is published within minutes of the Chancellor's speech starting in the House of Commons. A full report is available within a few hours. A great many organisations publish on the Internet and it is possible to download some of the information for perusal off-line.

Databases

Few individuals have access through their PCs to the ever-growing range of on-line databases, because of the cost. Access to these databases is gained via a PC with a modem and a telephone line. The user dials up the database in which they are interested, keys in a few words to instruct it to search for a given topic, and within a few seconds the database will respond with an indication of how much information it has found. The user can then have the information displayed on their PC, can download it to a floppy or hard disk, or can print the information on their printer. The user is normally charged for the amount of time they are connected to the database provider's computer, and for the quantity of information they extract.

Fortunately, more and more large reference and specialist libraries are offering an on-line database service which researchers can use on a one-off basis and be charged for the time and information accessed.

CD-ROM

This stands for Compact Disk Read Only Memory and is the technology which is currently having the most impact on the student consumer market. A CD-ROM is a plastic disk that looks very similar to an audio compact disc, but stores information rather than music. CD disks can hold vast quantities of information. One disk, for example, can hold the entire works of the *Encyclopaedia Brittanica*. The information can be accessed via a PC (personal computer) with a CD-ROM drive attached – a small box which plugs into the computer. Of course, CD-ROMs are only useful for information which does not need updating, for example standard reference books. On-line database are for current news and new developments.

Seven golden rules of research

Leave no stone unturned

If you do not ask, you will not know. Do not reject a possible research avenue just because it seems unlikely. What can it cost you? A phone call or a stamp maybe.

Copy faithfully

Never rush your research notes. Quotations must be totally accurate. Dates and places, sources, titles of books, year of publication – all these must be copied carefully and faithfully.

Check facts with other sources

Always double check with other sources any facts that come your way, particularly if they are verbal. If your research uncovers a dispute between authors or individuals over dates, times and places then make that clear in your submitted material, e.g. 'It is likely that the bombing raid on the bridge at Toulon took place on the night of December 4th 1941, but accounts differ by as much as two days'.

Attribute opinions accurately

When you come across a forceful opinion about some topic do not make it into your own, it could earn you a poor mark if the examiner/tutor disagrees. Make sure all opinions are attributed correctly to their sources, e.g. 'In the opinion of Dr Meyer, the benefits of a raised level of iron in the daily diet are greatly outweighed by the disadvantages.'

Keep a note of all source material

You must keep an accurate note of all sources of material – not only the names and titles of books, but which edition, which library and so on. This also applies to small documents, e.g. 'Letter from Mabel Watson to her son, dated 18th May 1875, from the estate of David Watson, deceased 1976. Now in the possession of the Geffrye Museum.'

Be generous with your research

The purpose of keeping accurate notes of all information is so your research can be passed on to others when you have finished. This form of generosity is how you came to be able to compile your material in the first place. So continue the academic tradition and help future generations of students.

Use your initiative

When you encounter one stumbling block, create a new opening. Sometimes it is difficult to find out about things, but with a little ingenuity and persistence you will be able to complete the task. Positive thinking produces positive results.

9   Information Storage and Retrieval

One of the most important elements in organising your programme of study effectively is to set up a system of storing and retrieving information. This means making sure you have a structured filing system that works for you.

There is no point in taking notes, carrying out research or writing essays, if you can't find the information later on when you need it. Your system should take care of notes, essays, research papers and, of course, computer disks.

Setting up a simple but effective system for storing and retrieving information will avoid the plaintive cry 'Now, where did I put that?' Start as you mean to go on!

What you need: files and somewhere to keep them

Cardboard files are made as wallets (which can be closed) or as folders. You may find the wallets safer for carrying notes around school or college, but the folders are easier to manage in a filing cabinet. If you buy your files pre-packed in bulk from a stationer they are not expensive.

Then make sure you have somewhere you can store your files safely – a filing cabinet if you have one, a couple of drawers in a dresser, or even a couple of large cardboard boxes. Make sure, too, that your disks are stored carefully in small boxes.

Organise your files

Think of the most logical categories for your files. Label all your files with the subject matter and the tutor's name. You may like to file by subject matter, e.g. Impressionist painters, Pre-Raphaelite painters, Cubist painters. Or you could label the files chronologically, e.g. 1800-1850, 1850-1900, 1900-1939.

Initially, put everything that is relevant into these files – notes, photocopies of articles, essays etc. Later you can sub-divide even further into smaller subject areas or time spans.

Make the effort to file things away every day, to avoid losing something that may eventually be crucial to your study plan.

Set up an index

You may find it helpful to number everything that goes in and set up an index as you go along so that you can find things quickly. This need be no more than a sheet of paper taped to the inside front of the file.

An index does not have to be detailed. If you give the first sheet of paper on a given subject a number, every other sheet of paper on that subject can be filed behind it and given a subsidiary code, e.g. Alexander the Great (first set of notes) can be indexed No. 1, with subsequent sets of notes called 1A, 1B, 1C or 1.1, 1.2, 1.3, or something similar.

In the index the subject matter of Alexander the Great is just given the number 1.

An index, can be done in two ways. You can list the subject matter alphabetically:

Alexander the Great	1
Babylonian Empire	23
Bolshevism	9
Calvinism	17
Christianity (Early)	12
Drake (Sir Francis)	7
Erasmus	3

Or you can list an index numerically:

1 Boron
2 Iron
3 Zinc
4 Magnesium
5 Calcium

The same goes for computer files. Of course, a computer automatically provides an index of sorts on each disk that you use, with the files, or subject matter, on each disk listed when the disk is first read.

Computers are here to stay

The use of computers is virtually mandatory in all study courses now and we are fast reaching the stage where tutors will ask for disks to be submitted for assignments rather than papers. However, speaking from personal and bitter experience, there are certain safeguards you must take to ensure that all your work done via computer is not lost or made inaccessible.

First, you must keep a disk and manual back-up of all your work. As soon as you have put data into the computer, whether it is basic notes, essays or theses, you must copy it on to a floppy disk and print it out and file it. Some people even keep a second back-up disk just in case, and keep the disks in separate places.

Secondly, you must save work and file on to the hard disk as you are working, so that if the computer should crash or there is a power failure, most of your work will have already been saved. Computers have an automatic save, but you can alter the time gap between auto saves; ten minutes is about the minimum you need.

Third, and this is particularly important if you are sharing a computer facility, either at home or at school or college, you must take care not to introduce any viruses into the system. Use only tested virus-free disks and make sure others do the same. If possible, do not allow your work computer to be used for playing computer games. It is often the introduction of cheap game disks that causes system problems.

Keep tabs on your research

A large part of your study programme will probably be devoted to research from books that you purchase or borrow or find in the library. If you find useful information and take notes, you must make a note of the reference source, so you can find it again if you need to.

A good way of doing this is to keep a card index system, again in alphabetical (by subject) order or chronological order, whichever is most helpful to you. Then when it comes to revision and you want to access and re-read this background material, you know where to obtain it quickly.

A typical card index system might read as follows:

Angina (causes of)

Pathology of modern medicine by Dr G. B. Masters (college library) pages 23-27

Heart disease in Western Society by Dr S. Lowe (borrowed from David Saunders) pages 19, 27, 84-86

Circulatory Problems by Michael Watson
BMA Journal No.189. 1995 (via college library)

Bulimia (treatment of)

Twentieth Century Eating Disorders
by Marjorie Wallace (Michaelson Library) pages 19-41

My Fight to be Thin by Angela Peters
Article in *The Independent*, 21 March 1995
(from college library) (whole book)

Progress in Treatment of Neurotic Conditions
by Dr H. Mannheim and Dr. K. Pew, Chapters 8 and 10
American Medical Journal, No. 887, 1995 (via town library)

10   Essays, Assignments and Presentations

Any large piece of written work needs to be properly structured and the foundation for the structure is all the notes, research material and other matter you have assembled. Knowing that you have all the facts and figures to hand and that you understand the subject matter thoroughly will give you the confidence to approach the task in a 'good stress' frame of mind.

First the plan

First you need to plan a skeleton structure for your work. You should already have your notes laid out in a logical flow of information. If not, now is the time to rewrite them so that they provide you with a proper *aide mémoire*.

Then you need to incorporate your research material into the plan that you are forming. This may be no more than notes within the notes which refer you to other material (see the following example):

Charles Dickens – His Formative Years

1. *Childhood*

    See notes on father.

    Also p.28 of Henry book.

    Quote of Mr Micawber here.

    See notes on mother.

    Also p.19 of Martin book.

    Incorporate photocopies of etchings here.

2. *Bankruptcy*

    See notes on family in debtors' prison.

    Also p.94 of Henry book.

Quotes from *Little Dorrit* here.

Insert material from Jack London's
Into the Abyss about child labour in London.

Quote from Dickens' diary about his own child labour
(p.72 of Collins book).

Incorporate photocopy of workhouse children photo here.

Quote from Dickens' daughter (p.65 of Hibbert book).

3. *The Young Man with a Career*

See notes on his first employment in a
solicitor's office.

Quote from *Bleak House* here.

See notes on new career as reporter.

Photocopy of engraving of the House of Commons
chamber here.

See notes on first Dickens' stories.

Quotes from *The Monthly Magazine* article.

First work as Boz (p. 25 Martin book).

Quote from *Greenwich Fair* story.

Here you can see an example of how, by organising all your basic material and working out the flow of information, the sources to be used, and any visuals to be incorporated, you have an excellent skeleton to which you can add the flesh. This method is used by professional writers the world over and is as successful for a 1,000-word essay as it is for a 150,000-word book.

The synopsis, or plan, that you have worked out, should then be read again, to see if you need to amend it by adding or taking away material, or changing the order of information. Once you are satisfied that you have a strong framework on which to build, you can proceed.

Working to a theme

You may have been given a theme to work to, or you may be asked to choose a theme. For example, taking the subject matter shown in the previous example:

Assignment

How did Charles Dickens' own childhood affect his writings? Discuss.

Assignment

Choose an aspect of Dickens' life and how it was reflected through his writings.

Let us suppose that, either way, your theme is to show that Dickens' own childhood, blighted by his father's debts and the need for him to leave school and go to work in a factory, influenced his choice of subject matter when he wrote his books in later life. You need to show the connection between Dickens' own feelings of horror and desperation at being forced into child labour (by quoting from his own diaries and letters) and the frequency with which he wrote about the London poor and child abuse by quoting from his books (*Oliver Twist, David Copperfield* etc.). You may also wish to bring in other material of the period which highlights the social problems of the day (such as the writings of Jack London, Octavia Hill, Charles Booth and others who were engaged in social observation and reform).

The crucial point is that you have a theme and all your efforts must be to stick to that theme and not deviate from it. The reader does not want to know about Dickens' love life, his houses, his taste in fancy clothes, or his travels to America. The reader wants to know, specifically, about his childhood and the effect it had on his later work.

At the planning stage you have to exercise your powers of discrimination by choosing and rejecting material that complements or detracts from it.

Stick to your theme, but do not labour the point. It is unnecessary to repeat the assignment sentence every few paragraphs, e.g. 'Dickens' own childhood experiences influenced his writing because...' The theme should be encapsulated in the title at the beginning: 'Dickens the Child Controlled the Man' perhaps, or 'A Childhood of Poverty Led to a Lifetime of Compassion'.

Using objective language

In Chapter 5, we talked about aiming for objectivity in your work. The purpose of presenting written work is to show how you are developing your abilities to understand subjects, analyse information, research details, separate theory, opinion and fact and develop a given or chosen theme. The word 'I' should almost never appear, unless you are writing about personal experiences. Your opinions count for nothing when you are a student, unless they are asked for. Even when they seem to be wanted, e.g. **Assignment** – 'What, in your opinion, is the prime purpose of children's television?' the person setting the assignment still does not want a piece of written work littered with the 'I' word. Look at the difference between the two arguments presented below:

Example 1: The prime purpose of children's television

While there is no doubt that children's television is there to entertain, I strongly feel that it should be there primarily to educate. I believe that, judging by the average child's response to television advertisements, most children regard television as more important than any of the other influences in their life. Therefore, with such power at their fingertips, television programmers should be compelled to regard the primary function of children's television as an educator.

A secondary function should also be to impart life skills – morals, behaviour patterns, speech patterns and so on, yet I feel that they are failing strongly in this area. Far too many programmes contain material which encourages children to lower their standards.

Example 2: The prime purpose of children's television

While there is no doubt that children's television is there to entertain, a great many people feel that it should be there primarily to educate. In a recent debate in London held by the National Union of Head Teachers, the majority voted overwhelmingly that, because of the influence television has over children, as observed through several classroom surveys conducted nationally, NUHT members felt that the prime purpose of television should be to educate, and they felt this motivation had been lost by television programmers.

Does this mean that children's television should be boring? 'Not at all', says NUHT spokeswoman, Laura King, 'All the pre-school programmes do an excellent job of teaching through play and fun; where it seems to fall down is in the older children's programmes. We want to see interesting and lively programmes for the over-eights which also contribute to positive life skills in the children, such as considerate behaviour and good speech patterns.'

Channel 10's Controller of Children's Programming, Simon Barnard, stated, however, in a recent article in *Television World* that 'Far too often blame is laid at the door of television for a variety of social ills, simply because other people, such as teachers and parents, refuse to accept their share of the responsibility'.

However, when challenged about the fact that many people feel that the prime purpose of children's television is to educate, he asserted that 'it does'. Even American cartoons? *Power Rangers? Biker Mice from Mars?* 'Even they teach the ultimate triumph of good over evil' he says, with as much conviction as he could muster.

Whilst there is nothing wrong with Example 1 – it contains well-constructed arguments – it nevertheless comes over as pure personal opinion, ready to be attacked by the first person who disagrees. Example 2 on the other hand, is also personal opinion, but is much more subtle. The argument is given a great deal of weight by using other people's opinions – those in authority – and both sides of the argument are presented, before the author subtly comes down in favour of the first argument simply by injecting a note of cynicism at the very end of the piece. Example 2 is much more difficult to argue against because the author's personal opinion has been bolstered by authoritative opinion from other quarters.

When you are asked for your opinion, what is really wanted is for you to present someone else's opinion, analyse it and agree or disagree. The use of objective language is important. Look at the following examples:

(a) It is thought by some experts, Stephen King in particular, that the universe has no boundaries – it is infinite. Most of us remain unconvinced, however, since the explanations for this new theory have proved unsatisfactory.

(b) Some people say that the true Cockney no longer exists, since most of the 'Cockneys' working in the East End actually live in Essex. Today, those more likely to be born within the sound of Bow bells are Punjabi or Bengali. Is this a racist view? No, merely a fact, gleaned from electoral rolls and parking ticket analyses.

To ally oneself with a group of people or a body of opinion is a good way of trying to be objective in a text. 'Some people say...' or 'Most of us remain unconvinced...' is preferable to using 'I'. Beware, however, that you can only get away with a few vague assertions of this nature. Most of the time you will be expected to state who holds the opinion and your sources.

Theories: substantiate them

Similarly, you must not make other people's theories, or even your own, into subjective opinions. If someone holds a theory that appeals to you, you must explain why, by analysing it fully and presenting the opposite view, to show that you are truly objective. For example:

Williams has a theory that maximum nutrition is achieved by the body only in its resting phase and therefore the most highly nutritious meals should be eaten in the evening when all strenuous physical activity has ceased. This is borne out by the many tests he has done on volunteer patients. All blood tests taken at regular intervals throughout the day and over a three month period show that those patients who followed his régime seemed to extract maximum nutrition from their food.

Many doctors dispute Williams' findings, stating that the experiments were not strictly controlled in the sense that everyone's body chemistry is so different you can only truly test such a theory on one person, by taking them from poor nutrition to maximum nutrition under strict control. Williams, however, argues that he has done this with several of his patients.

Criticism of a lack of controls in experiments is a typical response of traditional doctors to alternative therapists and should be discounted almost as a reflex negative response with no true analysis behind it.

Here the author has shown that they agree with Williams' theory by explaining the theory. Then the counter argument is provided and fully explained. Williams is allowed to respond, then the author dismisses the objections to Williams' theory as lacking in substance.

You have to try and be as objective as possible by presenting all the arguments; your eventual alliance with one side or another has to be fully explained, or you will lose credibility.

When propounding your own theories you have to work much harder to justify yourself. You have to explain the background to your thought processes, the investigations into the subject, any experiments you carried out, your findings and your conclusions. It helps to bring in the opinions of others particularly if they have done work which has prompted you to take a subject further.

Target your audience

Everyone does it. Shakespeare did it. He wrote to please the royal family (you only have to read his speech about Elizabeth I at the end of *Henry VIII* to realise what a creep he could be!). Here we are not talking about sycophancy, however (unless you have a tutor with a monumental ego that has to be pandered to in order for you to get good marks); we are talking about tailoring your work for a specific audience to gain maximum interest and maximum response.

Educators are supposed to be objective but they are only human and cannot always manage to completely set aside their own beliefs and prejudices. A friend of mine did a degree in political science and spent the whole course getting bad marks because his political bias conflicted with that of his tutor. If he had attempted to submerge his personal feelings a little and tailor his work towards the audience in question he might have had an easier passage through university.

We have talked about opinions and theories and how they can unbalance your work if you are not careful. Now we are talking about a little marketing – writing to please, to interest, to stimulate, to inform.

If you are just rehashing the same old tired stuff, without adding anything new, without presenting it effectively, then you will bore everyone and you will get low marks. The people who are teaching you, do the same thing year in and year out. A succession of students, perhaps even generations, have submitted the same papers about the same topics again and again. No wonder teachers and lecturers get frustrated. You have an opportunity to cheer them up a bit. Put some style into your work and make it a pleasure to read.

Watch your presentation

First loosen up a bit. You need to make your material highly readable without being too jokey, casual, pretentious or gimmicky. No slang words please. A good piece of written work has:

- a good flow of information
- does not stray from the theme
- uses short sentences and does not use ponderous language (in other words, reads more like natural speech)
- is broken up with headings, sub-headings, bullet points and visuals
- discusses a topic fully in each section and then leads the reader naturally into the next section
- is presented in a clear and easily readable font(some fonts are hard on readers' eyes)
- if possible, has colour or highlights to liven up parts of the work
- is presented clean, neatly bound and clearly titled, dated, attributed and **on time**.

You can use bullet points (as above) when you want to break a subject down into simple statements which can be referred to easily by the reader at other times. Check-lists can also be in bullet point form, or in tabular or question form. These are used when you want to recap the main points in a text. Summaries are lists or points at the end of a section or whole work that recap the main points of the preceding text.

Only use graphs, pie charts and flow charts if they are meaningful. Far too many people inject meaningless visuals into texts that add nothing to the reader's understanding of a subject.

Presentations

Presentations are becoming increasingly important nowadays as part of a course of study, particularly those with a teaching or business bias. A presentation is not a lecture or a lesson, although it should be informative. In the business world most presentations are instruments of persuasion. The more information you can give the audience about a topic and the more effective your presentation of that information is, the more likely you are to persuade them to a particular course of action.

There are several components to a good presentation and they must all be given equal weight:

- preparation
- delivery
- use of visuals
- the audience.

Preparation

A verbal presentation is prepared in much the same way as an essay. First map out the flow of information. Then collate your information. You need to write yourself a script, but this need be no more than key words or sentences on cards if your memory is good. You cannot possibly work without some kind of script because your audience is likely to be an interactive one. In other words, although they shouldn't, they might interrupt. So, even if you have learnt your presentation in the way an actor learns his script, the danger of interruption could throw you completely. On the other hand you don't want just to stand there and read a paper. The audience want to see you make eye contact with them occasionally, and preferably move away from the lectern or table now and then. For them to take an active interest in what you are saying, you need to be active too. This does not mean leaping around continuously or fidgeting – this is as much of a turn-off as someone who stands completely still.

You have to strike a balance between picking up the thread of your notes and making contact with your audience.

It goes without saying that you can only give an effective presentation on a subject with which you are totally familiar. You have to be prepared for any questions, interruptions or challenges.

A script, therefore, needs to be a memory jogger. It has to tell you what topic you should next address, when to use visuals, when to interact with the audience and so on. The following example shows how a script might run.

Presentation script

Opening
A few words of welcome and a brief explanation of the subject matter of the presentation, e.g. 'Good afternoon ladies and gentlemen. My name is Carol Smith and I am here today to talk to you about the recent progress made in the food industry, in particular, the subject of food irradiation, which I know concerns a great many of you. I hope that I can prove to you this afternoon that your fears are groundless.'

Place first visual on overhead projector
Note: the problem of the shelf life of food.

[You will now speak about this topic from memory, with perhaps the aid of a few notes.]

Place second visual on overhead projector
Note: the challenge confronting food technologists.

[This visual is a graph which shows the deterioration rates of various vegetables. This needs explanation and leads you on to discuss the problems that arise from this knowledge.]

Place third visual on overhead projector and hand out statistics to audience
[This visual is a copy of the information each member of the audience now holds in their hand. You explain the details of the information and add background material from your own notes.]

Pause and invite questions

[In this presentation scenario, the speaker has chosen to take questions at various points along the way, because the subject matter is complicated and requires complete understanding on the part of the audience before going on to the next part of the presentation.]

The speaker is using a mixture of notes and visual aids as her script. The visual aids act like bullet points in an essay; they focus the speaker's and the audience's mind on simple statements, which are then fleshed out by the speaker.

Delivery

There is a distinct difference between written English and spoken English, which is why it is not a good idea to deliver a paper. No matter how well it is written, it will always sound as though you are reading a document. There has to be some element of spontaneity in your delivery. That does not mean that you should devote the entire presentation to undisciplined, jokey banter. The odd piece of humour will not go amiss, but do not attempt it if you do not have the knack of comic timing!

When you have mapped out the skeleton plan from which you will work, it is good idea to rehearse and time it. Better to run short and make more time for questions, than to run on for too long and start everyone fidgeting. You may, in any case, have been given a time limit – a ten-minute presentation, for example.

Try to develop confident body language. The audience need to see your face, so pull your hair back, don't hunch your shoulders or bend down to look at your notes all the time. Glance down at them occasionally, and look out towards the audience, not being afraid to catch the eye of certain individuals in the process.

Your voice needs to be heard, so speak and stand with confidence. Do not mumble or pause too much. Do not 'um' or 'er' every other sentence, and smile occasionally if it does not conflict with the message you are delivering. As far as possible, try to relax.

Use of visuals

Visuals can be flip charts, photocopies handed out to the audience, slides projected by you on an overhead projector, slides controlled by you from a front-of-house or back-of-house projector, slides projected by someone else, a short film or a physical demonstration of an object working or an experiment taking place.

If you have the time, and, for example, you are not restricted to a ten-minute presentation exercise in class, always use some visuals. They help the audience to re-focus on the subject matter by changing their level of attention. They help to emphasise valuable points and help everyone's memory – that of the speaker and the audience.

The audience

All audiences have a limited attention span, which is why it helps to break up a presentation with visuals or, if the subject is complicated, to have several question sessions rather than one just at the end. No presentations are effective if they are just talk. Even radio broadcasts achieve variety by having sound effects, making part of the programme as an outside broadcast, or devoting some time to interviewing different people. An audience wants variety.

If the subject matter does not lend itself to visuals, then get others to help provide some variation. A presentation about the life of a politician, for example, might best be done by the main speaker providing a narrative, whilst others read extracts from letters, diaries and speeches, rather like a stage performance.

A presentation is, in effect, a performance and today's audiences are very sophisticated; television and cinema have made them impatient of less magical media. Therefore, you have to make some impact vocally, visually and intellectually, to gain their attention and keep it.

Do not forget that you can also use an audience to feed your presentation. Rather than giving examples yourself of the topic in hand you can throw this open to the audience, e.g. 'Can anyone give me an example of "Knocking's Law of Combustibles" at work in a daily setting?' Or you can set them tasks, e.g. 'I have just explained how the principle works. We will now have a ten-minute coffee break, and I would like as many of you as possible to write down examples of the application of the principle and hand them in to me before we resume'. This kind of participation keeps the audience interested and on your side.

Learn to be a critic and appraise other presentations, lectures and talks. Take on board their good points and resolve to eliminate the bad from your own work. After you have delivered a presentation, be objective about your shortcomings and try to improve the next time. Ask yourself questions – and answer them honestly:

- *Did the audience start fidgeting at any point during my presentation?*
  If the answer is 'yes', then maybe you should consider inserting some interactive phase at that point.

- *Did any of my statements cause the audience to react?*
  You may have wanted them to react, but if you did not then perhaps you should look at your choice of language. Are you being contentious instead of informative?

- *Did I run over my time?*
  If the answer is 'yes', did it matter, and if so, what can you cut out of the presentation without devaluing it?

- *Could I answer all the questions?*
  If you could not perhaps there is a gap in your knowledge. You should rectify this before you speak on the subject again.

- *Were the audience reluctant to ask questions?*
  This is a big problem. It can mean they are bored or do not understand the subject sufficiently to be able to ask questions about it. Ask for advice from an impartial observer or friend, and take steps to remedy it next time.

11 Memory Tips and Tricks

Some of us naturally have better memories than others, and generally speaking we find it easier to learn and memorise early in life rather than later. So, if you are a young student the chance are that your memory will be quite good. If you are someone returning to education after some years away and are out of the habit of studying, or are middle-aged and coming to this level of study for the first time, you memory is probably not as sharp as it could be.

Whatever our age or situation, however, we can all benefit from various tips and tricks to sharpen and improve our memories. Read on for some simple systems to help you remember.

Check your lifestyle

There is no doubt that basic improvements in your lifestyle can help your memory. Plenty of good-quality sleep, good nutrition, developing the ability to relax and organising your study will help you give your brain the best chance to function at top level.

Who's juggling?

Part-time students, especially those working and with families, probably have the biggest problem because they have far more disparate information cluttering their brains than full-time students, who are able to devote their brain's 'databanks' solely to their course. Trying to do a full-time job, be a parent and study is very difficult. It represents a lot of demands upon your brain for storage and recall of information. You have to remember everything that is required to function in your job; you have to remember everything that is required as a parent (who eats what, which child has a social engagement, which child has a dental appointment and when); and everything that is required for you to study. That is a huge amount of data. You cannot expect to be Mr or Mrs Memory Man all the time.

Short-term memory

There are things we commit to memory for a short period of time. We constantly make decisions about what is important. We remember an appointment at the doctor's for a short while, then we write it on the calendar or in a diary, then after it has passed, we forget about it. This is short term memory. This is why most people keep diaries, electronic organisers or use calendars. We need to write down notes to ourselves. There are certain things that our brain simply refuses to regard as important, which is why we forget. We all have short-term memory lapses – like walking into a room and not remembering why you came in, or your mind suddenly going blank so you can't remember a very familiar phone number. It is not just something that happens to the elderly.

Long-term memory

If you have had any experience of someone with Alzheimer's disease, the most frightening thing is that chronic sufferers eventually lose their long-term memory. In other words, they forget things they learnt as a baby, when they first began to develop their faculty for remembering, such as how to eat, or how to say basic words, things you imagine you could never forget.

As we get older it sometimes happens that the long-term memory improves and short-term memory declines. I remember more and more of my childhood, but cannot always remember easily what I did last week!

Study: a balancing act

The act of studying is a peculiar balance between short-term and long-term memory. For up to five years we may commit everything to do with our chosen subject to memory and be able to recall all of it at the drop of a hat. Five years after our study period is finished, we may remember very little of it, unless we have stayed within that subject area and continued to add to our fund of knowledge. I will give two friends of mine as examples. One studied anthropology and then went to work for a bank. She now remembers very little of her degree material. The other studied botany and went on to become a botanist. He remembers everything because he has continued to add to his knowledge. My banking friend has replaced her former fund of knowledge with a new one. Her brain has off-loaded what is no longer important.

Memory lapses: you can't remember or you don't want to?

Often the problem with our powers of recall is our subconscious desire not to remember. The brain is a computer which is programmed by us. If we are truly interested in a subject, our enthusiasm acts like fingers flying over a keyboard - we programme our computer brain with as much data as possible, which we can recall later. If we are bored, disinterested or confused, we send mixed messages to the brain, the data does not get stored in the part of the brain that is linked to efficient memory recall and we falter in our attempts to get it back.

Scientists have proved that the brain is divided into left and right hemispheres which each perform separate functions. The left side processes logic, words, lists, numbers, sequences, linearity and analysis. The right side processes rhythm, imagination, daydreaming, colour, dimension, spatial awareness and what is called 'gestalt', which means the whole picture.

It would therefore seem logical that each of us has a predisposition towards one side of the brain or the other. We all know of people who lean towards the arts or towards the sciences – those who have imagination and a feeling for colour and form and those who are skilled with numbers and sequences.

However, in the last 20 years, scientists have found that those people who use both sides of their brain together, seem to boost the ability of the whole brain. They have found that the study of music improves the study of mathematics and the study of languages seems to help the sense of rhythm.

It would seem, therefore, that the more areas of your brain you use to input data, the stronger the ability to recall will be. It would seem to be true that the more a subject captures your imagination (right side of the brain) the better you can analyse it and remember all the detailed facts and figures (left side of the brain). The less of your brain that is involved, when you are initially learning a subject, the less memory you will have.

Use all your senses

Today we have a great variety of teaching aids that stimulate the senses. How difficult it must have been to learn things by rote, with no television to look at, radio to listen to, tapes to play, pictures to look at or videos to watch. Children of five today are far more advanced than children of five were 50 years ago. Their senses are bombarded with new learning experiences every day and they absorb data at an exceptional rate.

The way to commit data to your memory banks is to use all your senses to absorb that information. Listen to a lecture, write notes, look at pictures, draw your own pictures, touch objects. Imagine you are studying art history. How dull and difficult to remember it would be if you learnt it all from books without ever visiting galleries here and abroad, without ever watching films about the lives of the great artists and where they lived and painted, without ever watching people put brush to canvas or hand to clay. Part of an effective learning process is to commit facts to memory along with personal experiences. We remember so much more the things we learnt with some emotion – excitement, interest, even disgust or annoyance – because, as scientists have proved, we are using both parts of the brain in the learning process.

A photographic memory

This specific phenomenon occurs in some people. It has been identified by scientists, who call it eidetic memory. It is the ability to remember in perfect detail anything that has been seen. Research suggests that it is usually a short-term memory phenomenon, although the men who made their living from their photographic memories in the music halls last century would seem to contradict this scientific assertion, since they could recall everything in perfect detail for periods of over 40 years.

If you are blessed with such a memory you can happily skip this chapter. Most people will have to read on!

Memory techniques: good or bad?

Many techniques supposedly improve your memory. The science of mnemonics offers such techniques as memory chains, telescoping, the link system, the Roman room system and so on. Some people find one or other of the methods useful, but there is often one major disadvantage – you have to re-programme your brain to the new system and this can completely throw out your natural memory abilities.

The Major System

Let us take an example. The Major System has been described as the 'ultimate basic memory system'. It was devised by a man called Von Wennsshein in the middle of the seventeenth century. The idea of the system is that it makes use of a different consonant or consonant sound for each number from 0 to 9 in a special code.

The Major System's special code

Number	Associated code
0	s, z, soft c
1	d, t, th
2	n
3	m
4	r
5	l
6	j, sh, soft ch, dg, soft g
7	k, hard ch, hard c, hard g, ng, qu
8	f, v
9	b, p

The vowels a, e, i, o, u and the letters h, w and y do not have numbers and are used as fillers in the Key Memory Image Words created. You obviously make up your own key words, but here I give an example provided by Tony Buzan in his book *Use Your Memory*, published by the BBC in 1986:

The Major System – Initial 100 Key Words

1	Day	27	Nag	53	Lamb
2	Noah	28	Navy	54	Lair
3	Ma	29	Nab	55	Lily
4	Ra	30	Mace	56	Lash
5	Law	31	Mat	57	Lake
6	Jaw	32	Man	58	Laugh
7	Key	33	Ma'am	59	Lab
8	Fee	34	Mare	60	Chase
9	Bay	35	Mail	61	Chat
10	Daze	36	Mash	62	Chain
11	Dad	37	Mac	63	Chime
12	Dan	38	Mafia	64	Chair
13	Dam	39	Map	65	Chill
14	Dare	40	Race	66	Cha-cha
15	Dale	41	Rat	67	Check
16	Dash	42	Rain	68	Chaff
17	Deck	43	Ram	69	Chap
18	Daffy	44	Rare	70	Case
19	Dab	45	Rail	71	Cat
20	NASA	46	Rash	72	Can
21	Net	47	Rack	73	Cameo
22	Nan	48	Rafia	74	Car
23	Name	49	Rap	75	Call
24	Nero	50	Lace	76	Cage
25	Nail	51	Lad	77	Cake
26	Nash	52	Lane	78	Cafe

79	Cab	87	Fake	95	Ball
80	Face	88	Fife	96	Bash
81	Fat	89	Fab	97	Back
82	Fan	90	Base	98	Beef
83	Fame	91	Bat	99	Baby
84	Far	92	Ban	100	Daisies
85	Fall	93	Burn		
86	Fish	94	Bar		

Therefore, if you wanted to remember the date 1776 you would now remember the associated keywords Deck/Cage. Does that help you?

The disadvantage seems to be – though everyone's brain works in a different way – is that you have to learn quite a complicated technique and submit that to memory as well as the other information you need to store and recall. You also have to add a translation skill to your brain's programme.

However, there are a great many memory techniques on offer, far too many to outline here. There are plenty of books on the subject, including others by Tony Buzan and Foulsham's *50 Best Memory Methods and Tests* edited by Julian Worthington (1996).

Rhymes

There are some simple methods to remember things, that we all learnt as children. For some reason the memory can recall rhymes better than straight facts. Perhaps it has something to do with using both parts of the brain. Rhymes are, of course, rhythmical, often humorous, and often provide a trigger for a good visual image, e.g. 'In 1492 Columbus sailed the ocean blue'. You can make up your own rhymes. They do not necessarily have to rhyme but they must have rhythm and sense. For example, the phrase we all use to remember how to adjust our clocks twice a year is 'Spring forward, Fall back'.

Acronyms

You can take the initial letters of keywords and make them into a word that helps you to remember something. For example, imagine that you want to remember this: 'The key factors in the rise to senior management are self-organisation, (the ability to organise oneself and others and set targets), image (the ability to recognise one's own image and improve upon it and to recognise one's interaction with the corporate image) and drive (the will and determination to succeed)'.

If you take the three key factors – self-organisation, image and drive – and take the three initial letters, they spell SID. A jokey acronym that helps you to remember quite a lengthy philosophy.

Association

Use the complete range of your mind to aid recall. We can make things more memorable by linking them with humour, colour, sounds, shapes, numbers, images, sizes. You have to find what works best for your mind and your studies.

A simple technique might be to colour-code various sections of your work. For example, if you were studying law you could do all civil law notes and research material on yellow paper, all criminal law notes on blue paper and so on. This may aid your recall mechanism. One student found that marking different material with triangles, stars, squares etc. helped her recall. She drew the shapes and coloured them in, bought packets of children's sticky shapes and stuck them on. It seemed as though the act of marking them in some way fixed the subject matter in her brain.

Re-reading and re-writing

Quite often, the reason that something gets consigned to our short-term memory and is easily discarded is because it is undemanding or was something with a limited life span. For something to be fixed in our long-term memory it has to be something that is done again and again.

You can aid your recall of subject matter by re-reading essays and books and by re-writing notes and essays. The more you go over a subject, preferably from different angles, with fresh viewpoints, the more you will remember. Remember, it is important to *write* as well as *read*, because you are using more than one part of your brain and are therefore raising the quality of data input and storage. So, read a topic and write a review of the book/chapter/essay/article as an exercise for your benefit only. This will stimulate different parts of the brain as you read, remember, analyse, write and appraise your written work.

Sometimes people will say 'I can always remember what I have written, I can just never remember what other people have written'. This is because when we put words down on paper, a whole range of senses and emotions come subtly into play, making the quality of data storage greater. Other people's words do not necessarily strike the same chords in our hearts and minds and therefore are not so easily accessed later.

On the other hand, there are occasions when other people's words move you so much that you have total recall of them for the rest of your life. Any actor who has played a major part in a great play will tell you that they remember every line that was spoken. In English literature classes students are rarely expected just to read Shakespeare's plays: it is part of the learning process to act them out. By acting, you experience the range of emotions the playwright wished to convey.

Games

A university tutor had a brilliant idea. He often played 'Trivial Pursuit' with his tutorial group, and noticed that the game was becoming stale because they had played it so often that most people had memorised the thousand or so answer cards. He therefore spent the whole of one summer vacation substituting the cards in a standard 'Trivial Pursuit' game with cards that covered every aspect of the course he was teaching. After initial reluctance, the students loved the game and said it improved their memories enormously.

I am not suggesting that you undertake such a Herculean task. The point is that game-playing is an excellent way to improve memory skills. If you and your friends can devise ways of testing each other's memories by creating games then you could liven up your revision programme quite a lot. Try the following:

Twenty questions
Each member of the group has to think of a subject. The others can

ask 20 questions that are designed to unmask the subject. For example:

Statement: A military man.

Rules: No one is allowed to ask the obvious questions, i.e. 'Is is Napoleon?'

Question: Is it a man who was born in Corsica?

Answer: No.

Question: Is it a man of the eighteenth century?

Answer: Yes.

And so on.

This game is designed to draw from the players their ability to recall facts that can uncover clues.

Snakes and ladders

Play with an ordinary 'Snakes and Ladders' board but make up a set of questions on your chosen topic. Before each player can go up a ladder they have to answer a question correctly. To save themselves from sliding down a snake they also have to answer a question correctly.

Picture time

You can do this with pictures, diagrams, any kind of printed visuals. Copy them, stick them on to card and cut them into eight random pieces. Divide players into teams of two. They have 30 seconds to assemble as much of the picture as possible and recognise what it is. If they can recognise it and explain satisfactorily what it is then they get 10 points. This game is apparently very popular with medical students, who need to be able to recognise parts of the body, organs, baccillus, and so on.

You can adapt any existing game into some method of memory test. It means that someone will have to prepare the questions, but perhaps you can take it in turns within your group of friends.

Give your memory a chance

Memory is a funny thing. For example, if you sit down quietly and make a shopping list before you go out, you remember everything you need and put it on your list. If you go round the supermarket

---

without a list, however, and try to remember what you need while being distracted by the sights and sounds around you, you invariably forget things and only remember them when it's too late. Why? Your brain has not changed in the supermarket. You know the information is there. It is because when you were sitting down there were no distractions and you remembered everything. The brain is a bit like a computer. When you are just doing one thing with it, it performs perfectly, but if you start to put data in one file whilst doing something else with another it falters a bit, or the printer stops for a few seconds whilst the programme switches between functions.

So, when you come to a test or examination, use your memory in the 'shopping list' way. Before you start to write the full answer to a question write down a list of the things you want to include in your answer on a spare piece of paper. Otherwise, later on, when your brain is trying to perform several functions at once – compose good written English, make a point, form arguments, draw upon examples – you will forget some the essential points you meant to include.

12 Need a Little Extra Help?

There comes a time when everyone flounders in their studies, if only for a little while, and needs some extra help. In Chapter 5 we spoke about the dangers of not being thorough when selecting your course and discovering too late that part of the course covered subject matter which is beyond your capabilities.

Most people have weak areas and it is good to admit to them. Don't try and cover them up and hope for the best. You need to confront your weaknesses and do something about them. Remember the two golden rules of studying:

- Most problems can be solved with a little time, work and patience

- If you come through this you will be a stronger and smarter person.

These may not be much consolation right now. But wait. Take a deep breath, relax and do not panic.

Do you really need help?

You are having trouble with your studies. You have to pinpoint exactly where the trouble is in order to arrive at a solution:

Statement: *I cannot do the work.*
Question: *Why?*
Answers: *(1)* *I don't understand it.*

(2) *I can't do it.*

(3) *I can't seem to get started on it.*

(4) *I don't know where to start.*

(5) *I can't get it done in time.*

(6) *I don't want to do it.*

All the answers given would seem to indicate a degree of hopelessness but, in fact only two of the answers truly indicate the need for extra help in the form of tuition. With the others the remedy lies in your own hands and no amount of extra tuition is going to solve matters.

Let's take each in turn:

(1) I don't understand it.

Here is a genuine need for extra help, whether in the form of shared study or formal extra tuition. Lack of understanding can have a knock-on effect, since most study programmes are formulated to progress naturally from one subject to another, through students understanding each phase and accumulating knowledge in stages. So, if you do not correct a gap in understanding, it will affect your ability to understand the next phase, and so on. Someone has to help you get over this crisis. Just who that person is will be discussed further on in the chapter.

(2) I can't do it.

This can mean several things – a genuine lack of ability, an unfounded fear of failure, or a temporary patch of self-doubt. Whichever one of these it is, you need to talk to someone about it – preferably your tutor. If you feel that the study programme is beyond you, you need to talk to the person who knows whether or not this is true. Only your tutor will be able to tell you honestly whether your fears are unfounded or whether you are, in fact, struggling, compared to the rest of the class. They will know, through experience, whether you can be helped by perhaps temporarily pairing you up with a more able student, or by transferring you to a less demanding course in your chosen field of study. There is another option, of course – giving up completely – but no tutor would recommend that unless it was patently obvious that you could not cope at all with any form of study.

If you say that you cannot do something because you have a fear of failure, and your tutor cannot persuade you that you will not necessarily fail, you must talk to a counsellor. A tutor may be able to talk you through a temporary patch of self-doubt so you will be able to resume your work with renewed confidence, but more serious psychological problems brought about by stress need independent help.

(3) I can't seem to get started on it.

This answer does not indicate lack of comprehension or ability but rather a lack of concentration. Serious lack of concentration, that causes you to admit defeat, can be caused by many things – tiredness, stress, relationship problems, illness – and pushing yourself even harder by seeking extra tuition, is not going to make the problem go away. You need to have a break and recharge your batteries – get lots of sleep, nourishing food, some relaxing company and activities, sort out your family and relationship problems, and get some medication and rest. Once you have cleared the decks and feel revived, you will find that your ability to concentrate comes back.

(4) I don't know where to start.

You have become disorganised. You are sitting down to prepare an assignment, but your notes are in a mess, or lost, you have not done sufficient research or background reading, and you do not know where to begin. Extra tuition is not going to re-organise your mind and materials. You might need extra help from a fellow student to replace the lost notes but, fundamentally, you just need to get your act together. You have to go back to a good system of detailed notes, an ordered system of keeping them and of doing thorough research.

(5) I can't get it done in time.

Your disorganisation goes hand in hand with a lack of time management. If you keep up a continual programme of organised planning, always working out how, when and where you are going to complete your next assignment, you will keep on top of things and never find yourself running out of time. Extra tuition is only going to eat into more of your scarce time. Cancel a few social commitments and make up the time you have lost. Get back on track with your time management and you can have a social life as well as a healthy study programme.

(6) I don't want to do it.

This is a bad case of boredom or rebellion, or both. It comes to us all at some point. The full-time student who has 'just had enough' (temporarily, we hope); the part-time student who just cannot raise the enthusiasm for the task in hand. Sometimes extra tuition can help, simply because a change of face and personality can re-awaken your interest in a subject. More often than not you just require a break – you need to be let out of the cage.

Sometimes this can happen on the last lap of a course, leading to exams; a small percentage of students misread what is a temporary condition caused by pressure of work and frustration as something more drastic, and elect to abandon all their hard work and refuse to take the exams. Talk to someone. Talk to students who are further on in their studies. They will reassure you that it is a phase that everyone goes through. Talk to your tutor and your family. Give yourself every chance to work it through without taking any drastic action. Extra tuition might help if it revives your motivation or speeds you through an unpalatable part of your course.

What sort of help do you need?

If you decide that you really do need extra help, then the next step is to decide what level of help is required. The options may be:

- family and friends
- fellow students at your level
- students at a higher level
- extra hours from your tutor
- evening classes
- summer and weekend schools
- private tuition.

Family and friends

Enlist the help of family and friends when you need to improve your organisation and time management. If you are trying to hold down a full-time job and study part-time, perhaps a family member could help you by putting your class notes onto computer for you to recall and edit later? Perhaps a family member could do your filing for you. Certainly they can help you to revise, get books from the library, seek out articles and photocopy them for you. If they are interested in your work, supportive of your aims and have the time, they would probably be only too pleased to help.

Good time management, as we discussed in Chapter 4, requires the co-operation of others to succeed. Have another talk with your family or flatmates. Explain your problems and see if they can help to give you extra time to study. If you can only find the extra time by cutting down on your social life, explain to your friends that you are retreating for a while but do not want to lose touch. Say that you will make up for it when your bad patch is over by throwing a party. That should also help your motivation!

If you are studying alone, get a family member or friend to help you raise the quality of your study by letting you talk things through with them. It may be a little above their heads but, gradually, they will come to understand some of your subject matter and be able to offer opinions or arguments. Certainly they should be there for you when you need to talk through any fears or anxieties.

Fellow students at your level

Your tutor may be able to suggest a fellow student who is sufficiently advanced with their studies to be able to help you overcome your difficult period of study. You may know someone yourself but it is doubtful whether you would have an objective enough view of their ability to teach you. A tutor would be more likely to know whether a fellow student is a good communicator and has the patience and interest to help someone else. You may be lucky and find that a fellow student and friend recognises that you are in difficulties and volunteers to help. If you are in a study group you have the ideal opportunity to confess your difficulties and ask for assistance from the others. However you get this level of extra help be aware that it can only be temporary, as others have commitments to their own studies and cannot support you indefinitely.

Students at a higher level

Help from this quarter may be possible, but it is usually the case that the further on in a course once progresses, the greater the pressure, and you may have difficulty finding a student at a higher level who can spare the time to assist you. However, they may be able to help in ways that are not too demanding of their time, such as lending you their past notes or essays to supplement your understanding of a particular topic. They may also be able to point you in the right direction to do some good research and you may be able to reap the benefit of their past research exercises.

Extra hours from your tutor

This may be a free service or a private arrangement. Obviously the course tutor is best placed to give you the extra tuition you need. They are acknowledged experts in the subject you are struggling to study. There are two obstacles to this perfect solution, however. One is that demands on the tutor's time may make it impossible for you to go down that avenue. The course may be particularly difficult, your intake of students may contain a high proportion of foreign students studying in their second or even third language – there could be several reasons why your tutor just cannot spare any more time. The second obstacle may be the tutor themself. They may be the reason why your studies are not progressing well. They may just be a bad communicator. It happens. They may have personal problems that cause the quality of teaching to drop temporarily. If this is the case you have no alternative but to seek extra tuition from another source until the problem tutor has ceased to be a problem.

Evening classes

It could just be possible that your subject is also being taught at an adult education institute somewhere and you could join the class for a limited period. This may not be satisfactory for certain subjects, since you may have to go over material that you are already conversant with. Where it can be valuable is as an extra source of practical experience, such as mechanics, science experiments, art, design, crafts, hairdressing, woodwork and so on. You may be weak on the practical side of your course because you do not get enough opportunity in your full-time class to practise your skills.

Summer and weekend schools

This is a popular practice in the USA. Students who want to gain extra credits towards their degree, or need extra tuition for part of their full-time course, attend summer or weekend schools, out of term-time. Many UK educational establishments now offer similar courses. They are structured mainly for external students but most have the facility, at a price, to take internal students too. Enquiries may reveal that, although your college is not planning a summer school in your particular subject, another college may be, and you can get a place on a one- or two-week residential course. It will not form part of your regular course fees, of course; you will have to pay an additional cost.

Private tuition

There are many individual private tutors and organisations who offer tuition, for a fee, on most subjects. Some are listed by the local education authorities, because they specialise in extra coaching to school-age students. Others are listed in the *Yellow Pages* or advertise in the local newspapers. It is best to choose one that has been recommended by a fellow student or by your educational establishment. It is impossible to say that this will guarantee value for money as the teaching process is so subjective. It involves the interaction of two personalities which may work very well for one combination of individuals but not for another. You may need to be bullied and intimidated into learning difficult subjects, others may need to be coaxed and cosseted.

Set your objectives for private tuition

It is worth mentioning that the cost of private tuition can always be shared. If a fellow student on your course has similar problems you might suggest that you share the cost of a private tutor. You can also ask the tutor or private college if they have any shared sessions. This may be more difficult to arrange, since it is unlikely that they will have someone with the same tutorial needs as yourself applying for tuition at the same time. However, it is worth enquiring.

Remember to set out your objectives:

*You must know what you need to learn and at what speed
you can realistically digest the information*

In other words you must privately set yourself and your new tutor some targets and ensure that they are met. You should be able to discuss with your private tutor at the outset what your learning requirements are and how they are going to structure your time together. If you feel they do not have a precise plan of work and are not setting their own targets, this tutor is not for you.

You must recognise the sort of atmosphere in which you can best learn

If you know that you have to have total concentration, freedom from distraction and complete organisation to learn, and you find yourself going for tuition to a brilliant but bumbling man with a house full of noisy children and a study overflowing with books and papers, then you must be firm with the tutor or tutorial organisation and say this will not work for you.

You must know when you are self-supporting again

You should know when you have met your targets, fully understand the subject matter and regained your confidence. Private tuition should not be an open-ended affair, it is too expensive. Use what you need and then call it a day.

How to get the best out of private tuition

Be active, not passive

Do not just sit there and listen – you might as well get them to send you cassette tapes if you are not going to participate. Ask questions, discuss topics. One-to-one private tuition is a valuable opportunity for airing all the doubts, problems and queries you may not get a chance to vocalise in a large group. It may be the very thing that has brought you to this need for extra help – the fact that, in class, you do not get the opportunity to re-examine subject matter because the others have moved on to other things.

Look for positive solutions

Do not spend your whole time with a private tutor being negative about your course. They know you have problems with your course, perhaps your class tutor, or perhaps your written work. Do not waste time moaning or criticising – be positive. You are there to overcome your problems, so get on with it.

Make the most of your allotted time

Prepare any questions you might have. Write them down and take them with you. Make good notes (see Chapter 7) and make sure there is some time at the end of the tutorial to go over your notes to make sure that you fully understand everything. Above all, arrive on time. If you only have a one-hour tutorial, it's a waste of everybody's time and your money if you persistently arrive ten minutes late.

Take some element of control

The tutor is there for you, and only you (unless two or more of you have elected to share a private tutorial). Therefore, within reason, you must have a hand in how the lesson is shaped. If you want to go over something again, insist upon it. If you feel confident that you understand a particular subject fully, then ask to progress to something new.

Organisational problems with extra tuition

Taking extra tuition will present you with an organisational problem. You could be going over old ground with your extra-curricular tutor whilst covering new ground in your class. This can add to your pressure and create a sense of confusion. It helps if you can take extra tutorials during half-term or end-of-term breaks, then you can catch up, in effect, before you tackle new material in class the next term. If your problems are greater than this suggested system can cope with, you may have to ask if you can go back a year, but this is for your college to decide.

Students studying by correspondence/distance learning have the advantage that temporary suspension of studies is an accepted practice if a student gets into difficulties. The student studying alone also has the freedom, of course, to keep going over information until they fully understand it, and is under no pressure from a fast class group.

Case history 10

The problem

Caroline is taking an external degree in economic history through one of the major universities in the UK. She has a full-time job and she attends two evening tutorials at the university a week. She has reached a patch, during her second year, where she is struggling to keep up. She is nearing the end of the year but is seriously worried about her ability to tackle the next year's work, given her poor performance this year.

The solution
After discussion with her tutor it is agreed that she will take two weeks holiday from her job and attend a summer school at the university to see if she can improve her understanding of the material. If at the end of the summer school, she has no more confidence, there will have to be a further discussion about her future studies.

Case history 11

The problem
Lionel has hit a low point in his college course because a whole term has been devoted to accountancy practices and this is his weak area. His flatmates, also on the same course, tried to help him, but the quality and quantity of their help was patchy and Lionel did not feel he was mastering the subject.

The solution
His parents therefore agreed to pay for a tutor from a private college that specialises in accountancy qualifications. He explained to the college exactly what coaching he needed and they were able to supply him with a tutor who would visit him at his home. After three months of private tuition Lionel is now able to keep up with the rest of the class in this subject area. Next term, the course moves away from accountancy and he will no longer need a private tutor, unless, when it comes to exams, he feels the need for some back-up for revision. But then it will only be for a limited period.

Case history 12

The problem
Evelyn is studying at veterinary college and generally doing very well. However, she lacks confidence on the practical side – particularly with her surgical skills.

The solution

After discussion with her tutor, he agreed to devote some time to supervising her, once a week, doing three or four post-mortems on a variety of animals. This additional practice, under supervision, was all that was required to develop her surgical skills to the point where she feels she is on a par with the rest of her colleagues.

13 Successful Revision

Revision is a fact of life – it has to be done – so you need to go about it in an organised, structured way, to make the best use of your time and the revision you do.

As with all the other elements in your studies, the ultimate objective is to work effectively towards success. Whether you already have some experience of higher-level studies, recently or some years ago; whether you are naturally well-organised person who finds it easy to plan; or someone who tends to leave everything till the last minute and indulge in frantic cramming, your approach to revision should be the same – to organise yourself and your work into a cohesive plan.

Your plan should answer these questions:

- what are the topics I need to revise?

- how much time do I realistically need to revise each topic thoroughly?

- what are my areas of strength/weakness?

- what should my revision priorities be?

This chapter will show you how to structure your revision and make the best use of your time and abilities. The following sample revision programme will give you a good basis for working out your own plan.

Sample revision programme

Home economics degree, year 2

11-week programme of revision

Examination week minus 11	Food and Nutrition *(Note: weak point: chemical interaction of foods in the body)*
Examination week minus 10	Product Development and Photography *(Note: weak point: market research techniques)*
Examination week minus 9	Human Resource Management *(Note: relate to topics in week -6)*
Examination week minus 8	Operations Management *(Note: weak point: logistics)*
Examination week minus 7	Marketing *(Note: weak points: pricing formulae and managing a mailing list)*
Examination week minus 6	Financial Management *(Note: weak point: restructuring overheads)*
Examination week minus 5	The European Consumer *(Note: relate back to marketing notes)*
Examination week minus 4	Food Retailing *(Note: weak points: product positioning and just-in-time management.* *Also: relate back to financial management notes)*
Examination week minus 3	Product Design and Evaluation *(Note: weak point: tactile psychology)*
Examination week minus 2	Health and Welfare *(Note: weak point: all the legislation!)*
Examination week minus 1	Read through all material again

Revision should be ongoing

It is bad planning to only revise at the end of a course, before an examination. Fortunately, most courses nowadays are structured around a continuous programme of assessment and testing, so it is difficult not to continually revise.

As explained in Chapter 7, revision begins when you revise your notes after a lecture. Read them, make sure you understand them, make sure all queries have been answered, and then make time after your class or lecture or when you get home to re-write them into clear and concise background material for your later use.

Revision must be proactive

Revision cannot just be the act of reading and hoping that your brain is retaining all the information. As explained in Chapter 11, good revision means exercising your brain's recall mechanism, by doing more than just reading. You have to write things out, vocalise them, discuss them. This is why, to revise properly, you need help from others at some point.

How to revise: one method is not enough

Using old exam papers

Using old exam papers is an excellent way of testing your comprehension and recall of a subject. It is not necessary to write fully-fledged essays as answers. You can write abbreviated notes, as long as you know that you could flesh them out if you needed to. The point of testing yourself with old exam paper questions is that they provide totally objective memory jogs.

They are also an excellent method of highlighting strong and weak areas in your knowledge and this helps you to consolidate your revision plan. Any questions you find difficult to answer show that you have an area of knowledge that needs boosting. These are the subject areas that require extra revision on your part.

Using textbook exercises

Most textbooks have exercises in recall and presentation of information at the end of each chapter. Use these. They are most useful as part of a continuous revision programme because they are intended to be used immediately after you have learnt a new chunk of information.

Setting your own exercises

One of the most successful ways of revising a subject is to take the subject matter apart and re-assemble it in a variety of ways. This helps you to learn a subject inside out, to expand on it and be able to summon up your recall of it, no matter from which direction the question comes.

One way to do this is to take one of your essays, read it through, then think of three ways in which you can approach the subject from a different angle. You may, for example, have written a piece about 'The Fall of the Napoleonic Empire'. Read it again and see if you can find three different angles from which you could rewrite the material and expand it to include other areas of your knowledge.

Look at the following example:

An extract from *The Life and Times of Napoleon*, published by Hamlyn, 1967:

'There are still many pages missing in the Napoleonic epic, but it is not too early for a summing-up. French schoolbooks teach that Napoleon's glory cost France the loss of her natural frontiers, vast sums of money, an appalling number of lives. True. From the French point of view the Napoleonic age was indeed a costly one. But his role transcends mere national boundaries. Napoleon, and the Revolution of which he was the product, cannot be considered from an exclusively French point of view. From a European standpoint, the benefits he bestowed upon the then 'emerging nations' were incalculable, albeit often involuntary.

His passion for centralising and unifying gave impetus to the reshaping of old Europe that continued even after his downfall. Although he had tried to suppress in France many of the principles set forth by the French Revolution, he spread those principles elsewhere in Europe, notably in Spain, Germany and Italy. His last wish would have been to promote a united Germany, yet his reduction of the number of fragmentary

German principalities was to do just that. Nor did he have any desire to unite Italy; yet by giving the Italians a taste of national independence he set their unification in motion. His brutal and senseless oppression of the Spaniards aroused in them a burning nationalism.

By his victories and conquests he demonstrated the rottenness of the old order and the need for reform, and his unfulfilled promise to 'liberated' lands gave them a taste of freedom which spurred them to greater nationalistic and united efforts. His very insensibility and the oppressive measures he took against them spurred them to action and gave them a sense of dignity and importance that no mere decree could have done. His shabby treatment of the Pope gave the Church a moral authority such as it had not had for centuries. His greatest wish had been to strengthen his own imperial power, yet by treating kings as though they were clerks, by showing up the moral decay of European sovereigns, he dealt the final blow to the European monarchy.'

Here we have a piece on the legacy unwittingly left by Napoleon. Imagine that it is one of your past essays. Read it through and find three different angles from which to rewrite the subject matter. Perhaps the following:

(1) Explain the effect that Napoleon had on the eventual unification of Germany.

This gives you a chance to rewrite and expand upon the material you have, drawing on your further knowledge of other material.

(2) Discuss how Napoleon abandoned the principles of the French Revolution.

(3) Discuss the position of the Church during Napoleon's lifetime.

Writing book critiques

As part of your on-going revision programme, fix knowledge that you have acquired from books indelibly in your brain by writing critiques of those books. Analysing, appraising or criticising a book is a way of making information easy to recall. It also develops your ability to discuss on paper options, opinions, arguments and counter-arguments.

Revision is not just learning facts and figures

Post-GCSE revision means more than the mere recall of information. Revision at a higher level means revising your skills as well as your fund of knowledge. Over your course of study you will, it is hoped, have developed your ability to discuss, analyse, argue, develop points, construct themes, and so on. Honing these skills is as important as knowing the information that you have to manipulate.

Thus, revision cannot just mean memorising dates, facts and figures. Of course, that is part of your revision plan. However, you should also be setting yourself skill exercises – refining your ability to recall information and present it in whatever way is demanded.

This is where all the suggestions we have considered come into play. Using old exam papers, textbook exercises, developing your own exercises and writing critiques are all methods of recalling and re-presenting information in different forms.

Revising with a tutor

Most tutors should allow time within classes and course structures to revise material. This can take the form of regular test papers, classroom discussions or revision assignments. From the tutor's point of view, there has to be some element of revision which 'puts you on the spot' – in other words, which simulates exam conditions in some way either by expecting you to recall and present information without the help of textbooks and notes, or by expecting you to do so within a time limit.

No amount of revision at home is going to prepare you for the lack of background material support that confronts you in an exam room. So you, as well as your tutor, have to set yourself revision exercises where you rely solely on your memory and your presentation abilities, with no back up.

Revising in a group

If you are part of a study group then you should have regular revision sessions. Sometimes these can be planned subjects, e.g. 'Next week we are going to discuss VAT. So revise that topic', or they can take the form of 'spot checks' where a subject is discussed without any warning and puts everyone on the spot.

Spot check revision method for a study group

The group agrees that each week everyone will write down on a piece of paper a topic that they would most like to revise through discussion. Most people will pick one of their weaker subjects because they would like the help of the group in tackling that subject matter. All the pieces of paper are then put in a bowl, like raffle tickets, mixed around and one is picked out. The subject for that week is therefore chosen.

Revising with a friend

If the person helping you is a fellow student on your course then the way in which you approach your joint revision can be quite detailed. Their level of knowledge means that they can set you questions, lead your train of thought, correct you and stimulate your memory.

If you make it a two-way process, with each helping the other, it adds to the quality of revision. Giving knowledge to someone else is a great way to improve your own level of knowledge. It is a more relaxed way to revise, and you are using all your senses to aid your memory: writing, speaking, listening, watching.

Revising with your family

This is more difficult and not so productive. When you use someone who does not have your level of knowledge to help you revise, it limits you to mere recall of dates, facts, figures, names, translations etc., the 'learning by rote' things that can be listed and given to your relative to test you with, or read from a book.

You could, of course, be extremely lucky and be studying a subject in which one of your parents or your partner is already qualified. What luxury to be studying medicine and have a qualified doctor for a parent/partner! You have a constant source of revision. However, I suspect any parent or partner who qualified a long time ago (or even fairly recently) may have forgotten quite a bit, so do not expect revision to progress smoothly!

Revising alone

Do not despair if you have no alternative but to revise on your own. It has many advantages, the main one being the facility to concentrate totally on what you are doing. Providing you give yourself plenty of variety in the way that you revise, i.e. read, write, set yourself tests, analyse written matter, keep fact lists in your pocket and look at them from time to time, then you should manage perfectly well.

It is easier to get bored or tired if you are working alone, because you have no companion to stimulate you or push you on. So break up your revision periods into short sessions, to be tackled when you are feeling energetic and your brain is lively. Do not attempt revision at the end of the day when you are tired, except to read a short amount of material at bedtime.

Revising specifically for exams

Set yourself a timetable

It is important that in your final stretch before exams you set up a revision timetable, in plenty of time, so that you know you will be able to cover all the subjects you need to cover and how much time you must allocate for each subject (see the sample timetable on page 126). In your timetable, make notes to yourself about subjects which need special attention or those that relate back to other sections of your course. Then you will make sure that you do not miss out anything that is important and can allow yourself extra time for the most difficult subjects. Work steadily through the programme you have set yourself and allow yourself some time at the end to go through it all again.

Don't leave it all till the last minute

If you leave all your revision to the last couple of weeks, you will find yourself glossing over certain subjects because you have run out of time. This is when panic sets in.

The worst way of pre-exam revising is to work around the clock, neglecting sleep, food and drink. Not even the very young can keep up that sort of schedule for long and you are only ruining your chances in the examination itself. Your memory stands a good chance of failing you completely if you are too tired to summon it up.

If you revise continually, throughout the year, pre-exam revision should only be a top-up. If you set yourself a timetable, you may actually be able to afford a couple of days off for relaxation before the exams start. You are aiming for a feeling of relaxed confidence when you enter the exam room and this can only be achieved by measured work over a reasonable period of time.

Cover your bets

Never be convinced by others, even tutors, that there are certain subjects that will not crop up in the exam and certain subjects that always do. You could just be unlucky and discover that half your marks have gone before you start because this year they have decided to ask questions on the three subjects you neglected to revise. Many people get past examination papers and convince themselves that there is a pattern to the questions asked. Your chances of being able to predict accurately what your examination papers will contain are about the same as your chances at roulette. It is best not to gamble but to cover all your bets by knowing all your subjects thoroughly. Then you can enter the examination room with confidence rather than trepidation.

Stress control: the pre-exam checklist

Don't

- rely on past examination papers as a guide to what will or will not be asked

- leave all your revision to the last couple of weeks before the exam

- gloss over certain subjects because you have run out of time and patience

- skimp on sleep or food.

Do

- work out a specific revision timetable
- set yourself exercises that make maximum use of your knowledge and skills
- seek help in your weak areas of knowledge
- set yourself timed revision exercises that simulate exam conditions
- give yourself rest from revision work
- get plenty of sleep and good food
- cut down on socialising and alcohol.

14 How to Cope with Exams

As we discussed in the last chapter, the best way to enter an examination room is with a feeling of quiet confidence. This can be achieved by being happy about your level of knowledge, and you will, it is hoped, have achieved this through having carried out sensible and thorough revision.

Confidence is the aim

There are other factors which can contribute to a feeling of confidence:

- Relaxation
- Absence of nervous tension and irritability
- Lack of personal problems and distractions
- Feeling of well-being
- Lack of negative thoughts
- An understanding of the exam procedures and rules
- Confidence that you have the necessary materials for the exam
- Comfort
- Confidence about the time, place and duration of the exam.

Relaxation

We start with this, although it really only comes from getting all the other points listed above sorted out. Relaxation comes from knowing that you have organised yourself, your thoughts and your actions, and have nothing to worry about except completing the examination.

Absence of nervous tension and irritability

You should only experience good stress in an examination room: the stress that comes from the surge of adrenaline as you rise to the challenges presented to you in the exam paper.

It is natural for most people to approach examinations with feelings of anxiety and tension. You can eliminate most of these by knowing that you have done the work as thoroughly as you can. Any residual tension can be dissipated by physical exercise (not too much or you will exhaust yourself) and laughter. The day before your exam, take the day off from revision. Last-minute cramming will only heighten your tension. If you plan to have a quiet day at home, watch a comedy video, have friends round for lunch or coffee, go shopping for a 'reward', anything that takes your mind off the impending exam and gives you the opportunity to laugh and relax.

Lack of personal problems and distractions

You have to enlist the help of family and friends to get you through the examination period. They must appreciate that now is not the time to pick a fight with you about something, make demands on your time and emotions, create problems in general or give you a hard time.

Spouses/girlfriends and boyfriends have to back off and tread on eggshells during examinations. Your ego is very fragile and your state of mind precarious. You must impress on them that all decisions, commitments and entanglements have to wait until after the exams to be sorted out.

Children have to be told to respect your needs during this time. Unco-operative teenagers may even have to be grounded so that you don't spend the night before your examination waiting up until the small hours for them to come home. Explain to them that you co-operated when they had exams – now it's their turn.

Disasters in the home have to be dealt with as speedily as possible with the minimum amount of fuss. You have to put your hand in your pocket and pay for a 24-hour plumber to come out rather than sit through your exam wondering whether your home is going to be flooded when you get back.

Serious personal problems, such as severe illness or an accident in the family, can impair your ability to concentrate so much that you may have to back out of the exam and resit. Better that than struggle with feelings of guilt and worry and turn in a sub-standard exam paper.

Taking an examination is, of necessity, a selfish act. You have to put yourself first. Sometimes this means removing yourself from domestic hassle altogether and going to stay somewhere alone in the week leading up to the exams.

Feeling of well-being

This can only come from treating your body and mind well. No late nights – plenty of sleep is important. If you are having trouble sleeping get some of the over-the-counter herbal remedies to help get you through the bad patch. Try to avoid prescribed drugs as many of them leave you with a 'hangover' the next day and you do not want to have to struggle with that in an examination.

You must eat well. That does not mean heavily. Nutritious light meals are ideal. Nervousness can make your stomach reluctant to accept rich foods, and certainly on the day of an exam it is best to have a light breakfast, otherwise you may feel sleepy. A little bit of hunger keeps you alert. But again, not too much hunger. If your blood sugar gets too low you will start yawning. Most examination boards will allow you to take in a small snack, like a chocolate bar, biscuits or a sandwich, which should be clearly visible on the table, for you to eat during the exam.

Do not drink too much tea or coffee before an exam. You do not need stimulants of any kind. Besides, you do not want to have to keep popping out to the toilet during the exam; it takes too much time, and anyway, it's probably not allowed!

Do not drink alcohol the night before. It clouds the brain the next day, not to mention destroying brain cells (and can you honestly afford to lose any at this particular moment?). Don't eat exotic foods, like curries, either, which may have a laxative effect just when you do not need it!

Make sure that you do not forget any regular medication that you need. Pre-exam nerves can make you forget the most regular of daily tasks. If periods of long concentration are liable to give you a headache, take a couple of headache pills into the examination room with you, in case you need them. However, be sure to inform the invigilator before the examination starts.

Make the day before the exam a relaxing one. Do not overdo exercise or go on a marathon shopping spree. You do not want aching muscles or sore feet to distract you during your exam.

Lack of negative thoughts

You must banish these from your mind. Even if you have not prepared yourself as well as you should have done, do not allow yourself to dwell on your shortcomings; think only about your positive points. Do not brood over what will happen if you do not pass this exam or exams. Think only of the exam ahead of you, and the work you have to do.

Instruct those around you to offer only positive thoughts. You want to go out of the door to cries of 'Good Luck!' and 'You won't have any problems!' not to phrases like 'Never mind, dear, it doesn't really matter if you don't pass' or 'You can't help exam nerves, your father was the same. He knew everything, but he could never pass an exam'.

When you get to the place of the examination, avoid getting into conversations with others in case they start being negative and dragging you down. Try not even to eavesdrop on conversations. The last thing you need five minutes before you go in is to hear a fellow student saying 'Jenkins sat this exam last year and it was so hard his year only managed a 30 per cent pass rate'.

An understanding of the exam procedures and rules

Well before the examination takes place make sure that you understand and make a note of the rules governing the sitting of the exam. You need to know what you are allowed to take in to the exam, e.g. calculator, ruler, dictionary, drink, snack etc. You must know the procedures if you need to ask for more paper, to go to the toilet, if you do not understand a question, if you find a mistake in the paper and so on. You need to know how the paper will be constructed. Will it, for example, be in three equal parts, each giving the same amount of marks? Or will it be a multiple-choice paper with no requirement for essay-type answers? Will there be an oral examination? Will you lose marks for messy writing or not numbering the pages? Will you get marks for showing how you worked out a formula, even if the final answer is not right?

Confidence that you have the necessary materials for the exam

Find out what you need and then make a list. Pack these into your bag the night before, ticking off the list as you go. Make sure you remember to take the bag with you!

Apart from packing items to assist you in the presentation of your written material, you may need medication, a snack, a drink, spare pens and pencils, a handkerchief, your spectacles or spare contact lenses – put them all on your list.

Comfort

This can embrace several things. First, clothing. It is important to wear comfortable clothes and shoes. Underwear that is too tight, jeans that cut into your stomach, a sweater that is too hot – all these trivial matters will become sources of intense irritation and distraction during a long examination. Your circulation will be affected by a long period of sitting down, so do not add to it by wearing clothing that is too tight around your lower body. You may also feel too hot or too cold because of the temperature of the room, or because sitting and concentrating for a long time has actually lowered your body temperature. It is best to plan for this by wearing layers. For both men and women it is advisable to go into the exam wearing loose, comfortable, lightweight clothes. You should have additional items to hand if you feel cold, such as a jumper and a pair of socks.

Comfort also means dealing beforehand with any aches and pains that could cause you discomfort during an exam – your pulled shoulder muscle, your aching back, your sprained ankle. Take painkillers about half an hour before the exam. Rub your aching muscles with an odour-free liniment, please (think of the students around you!). Strap up your sprained ankle. Ask the invigilator for a stool to rest your injured leg or foot on if it starts aching, but ask for it before the exam starts, so that it can be found and put in place in time. Or bring your own, if you are coming by car.

Find out beforehand, if you can, what the examination room and the seats are like. If you know that sitting down for a long time on a hard seat is going to make you very uncomfortable, then bring along a cushion.

I may have painted a picture of a student who turns up with everything but the kitchen sink in order to take an examination but, obviously, there are limits. No invigilator is going to be able to cope with a student who struggles through the door with their own reclining chair and a picnic hamper!

Confidence about the time, place and duration of the exam

Make sure that you know the exact time, place and duration of the exam. This may be an obvious point, but it is suprising how many people turn up late because they thought the exam started at half past two and not two o'clock, or go to the wrong building, or even turn up on the wrong day. Check, check and double-check.

Find out how long the exam will take. You need to check this a long time before the exam otherwise you cannot set yourself accurate revision tests in the lead-up to the exam.

Make sure your transport arrangements to and from the exam are well organised. If you have to take public transport, allow for delays and cancellations. Even if you are planning to go by car – either driving yourself or being given a lift – find out about public transport in case there are last-minute problems with the car. Set off by car in good time to allow for traffic hold-ups and the time it takes to find a parking space. Find out beforehand where you can park and, if there is not a free space, don't park on a meter because you will not be able to pop out of the exam to top it up!

Stick a note on the dashboard of your car to remind you to take everything you need out of the car. Last-minute exam nerves can make fools of us all.

Plan to get to the place of the examination early. It is better to be too early and to go for a cup of tea whilst you wait than to put yourself in a state of panic because you have only minutes to spare or are late.

Coping with practical examinations

Make sure you fully understand what materials and tools you need to take to a practical examination. Are you allowed to use your own paintbrushes, or do you have to use theirs? Are you expected to provide swatches of fabric or will these be available? Can you take your own toolbox along, or do you have to use the college's? Will models be available or do you have to arrange your own? And so on.

Examination techniques

- Read through the whole paper first
- Make sure you fully understand the questions
- Take note of any advice given on the paper
- Use your spare paper to map out your answers
- Follow presentation instructions
- Answer the easiest questions first
- Tackle the remaining questions
- Mark off the questions as you answer them
- Use any spare time to check your work

Read through the whole paper first

Read the paper thoroughly first so that you can map out your plan of attack. You may find, for example, that a topic is split over two questions, and if you do not read the whole paper first you may find that you have confused matters by giving the whole answer in the first question and have to write it all out again, splitting it into two.

Example:
Question 1: Why was Thomas Hardy able to relate to nineteenth-century readers so effectively?

Your answer gives a detailed account of his childhood and personal experiences which enabled him graphically to describe rural life in the early nineteenth century; his readers therefore found it very topical.

However, later on you come to:

Question 7: Explain how Thomas Hardy's childhood and personal experiences surfaced in his writings.

You, of course, have already covered that ground in Question 1. Now what do you do? Waste valuable time by rewriting Question 1 or lose marks by feebly writing 'See Question 1' where the answer to Question 7 should be?

Now you see the value of reading the whole paper through before you start.

There is another point. It has been known for exam papers to contain mistakes – grave printing errors which affect the outcome of the exam. You want to find that out before you proceed. Put up your hand and point it out to the invigilator.

Make sure you fully understand the questions

You need to be sure that you are giving the examiners exactly what they have asked for. If they ask you to compare, do so; do not discuss or analyse. If they ask you to list something, that is what they are expecting you to do – to construct a clear and concise list and not to waffle on about irrelevant matters. See the glossary of examination terms at the end of this chapter.

If you really do not understand the construction or sense of a question, raise your hand and ask the invigilator. Do not be embarrassed about it. It could be one of those printing errors mentioned above and if you do not draw attention to it you will severely handicap your chances of completing a good paper.

Take note of any advice given on the paper

It may be that there is an explanation of the number of marks allotted to each portion of the paper and a recommendation as to how much time you should devote to each section. There may be other instructions about what the examiners want to see, e.g. they do not want you to work out all your calculations on a piece of spare paper, but they want to see all your calculations on the main paper. Read and make sure you fully understand all these instructions before starting.

Use your spare paper to map out your answers

If you spend just five minutes writing out notes on the flow of information for each answer, you will ultimately save yourself far more minutes in thinking time. When you have read the paper through and decided which questions you are going to answer, write down on your spare paper some quick notes to yourself (as was discussed in Chapter 7) showing how you think the information should flow and points you want to make sure you remember to include. Also quickly jot down any dates, formulae, names, quotes etc. Do this now, while you remember them, in case you have a memory blank later on through tiredness. These notes will be invaluable in keeping your mind on track and allowing you to write speedily and with confidence.

Follow presentation instructions

Again be sure that you have read the whole paper and any attached notes. If the examiners want no writing in the margins, make sure you observe that instruction. Take note of whether they want every page numbered, and also whether they want your name at the top of every page. They may want you to start each question on a fresh page, and not to carry on under the last question. They may insist that all calculations or underlinings are in a different colour pen from the main body of text. There could be many instructions to be heeded. Do not ignore them because that will almost certainly cost you marks – admittedly not many, but who can afford to throw away even a few?

Answer the easiest questions first

It is usually perfectly acceptable to answer questions in a random order. You need to get as many marks as you can in the time allowed. It is better that you use the time efficiently to answer questions that do not pose any problem, rather than waste a lot of time struggling with the really difficult ones.

Tackle the remaining questions

Look at those questions you have left and, if possible, make the following judgements:

- Select the questions that carry the most marks and use your remaining time answering those.

- If you are faced with a question to which you know half the answer, do what you can. The examiner will assume you have run out of time and you will at least get some marks.

If you are very short of time and you still have an essay question outstanding, write: 'Please note that I have run out of time and therefore cannot answer this question in full. I am therefore giving you a list of the salient points to show my understanding of the question and subject matter'. Then do a list of the main points of the answer, in logical progression, as though you were drawing up your information map for the full essay answer. You may get some marks for effort and understanding which is better than none at all.

If, for any reason, you do not understand a question, or you strongly disagree with it, write an explanation of your lack of understanding or your annoyance. It may be ignored but, on the other hand, you may be communicating a valuable point. Never waste an opportunity to communicate.

Mark off the questions as you answer them

It may seem an obvious point but it is amazing how many people, in a state of exam nerves, completely miss out questions. Tick off each question as you have answered it, then there can be no mistake.

Use any spare time to check your work

No matter how well you think you have done in the exam and how fast you have completed it, **do not leave early**. Spend any spare time checking and re-checking your work. Perhaps, as you are now more relaxed, you will think of things that you have missed or, as you read through your work, you will find some writing that is illegible or sentences that are badly constructed. You are now in the fortunate position of being able to correct them.

When the exam is over

By all means let off steam, go for a drink, have a good time, but try to avoid conducting post-mortems on the exam itself. There is no point in brooding about your performance or allowing others to make you depressed by going on and on about the toughness of the exam. Besides, the chances are that you are caught up in a series of exams over a period of a week or two and you need to maintain a state of equilibrium until the final exam is taken. Just carry on with your routine, look after yourself physically and mentally and keep control.

Glossary of examination terms

Account (give an)
This may be qualified by the term 'brief', i.e. 'Give a brief account of the rise to power of the Nazi Party in the early 1930s'. Giving an account is merely a detailed description of a subject without any analysis, opinion, discussion or debate.

Account (for)
E.g. 'Account for the decline in the strength of sterling in the latter half of 1985'. This means give the reasons why such a thing happened.

Analyse
E.g. 'Analyse the success of the automotive industry in Japan'. This instruction requires you to examine and discuss the various components that have contributed to the success of this industry, and to put forward opinions, your own or others', as to why this success occurred.

Appreciation
E.g. 'Write an appreciation of the work of Linus Pauling'. This does not mean praise, but it means give a balanced judgement of the man's work.

Assess
E.g. 'Assess the value of De Gaulle's contribution to the European Economic Community'. This means examine and put a value on his contribution.

Characterise

E.g. 'Characterise the values of western religions'. This means outline the typical features of all the religions. It does not mean compare or analyse. It is a straightforward request for information.

Comment

E.g. 'Comment on the marketing philosophy of the food industry'. The world is your oyster. You can criticise, analyse, discuss, do anything really, but make sure it is supported by informative facts and figures. No examiner wants pure opinion.

Compare

This invites you to take two or more topics/philosophies/opinions/works and find their similarities and differences.

Contrast

This, on the other hand, invites you merely to find the differences between two topics.

Consider

E.g. 'Consider the role of women in Alan Ayckbourn plays'. An invitation simply to discuss and present your opinions based on your findings.

Criticise

E.g. 'Write a critical piece about tabloid newspapers'.This is self-explanatory really; you are being invited to make constructive and reasoned criticism of the subject matter, to denigrate it, whilst being able to support your feelings with material from other sources, if possible.

Define

Usually means to explain what something means - usually a piece of jargon, e.g. 'Define the term 'networking'.

Demonstrate

Means 'Show me what you have found out and how you can use it to support your argument', e.g. 'Demonstrate the usefulness of carbon in manufactured products'.

Describe

A perfectly straightforward request that requires a straightforward answer. If you are asked to describe something, stick to the facts; do not stray into areas of poetic description. The examiner just wants to know if something is orange, not that it 'glows the colour of the sun dying at the end of the day'.

Discuss
An invitation to debate a topic by showing the variety of arguments and opinions you have absorbed and bringing the whole discussion to a logical conclusion.

Estimate
This usually means 'How important is (something)?', e.g. 'Estimate the importance of air travel in the development of international communications'.

Examine
A request to investigate a topic in detail, e.g. 'Examine the causes of black holes'.

Explain
Another fairly straightforward instruction, but do not regard it too simplistically. To explain something requires a certain amount of deductive reasoning and analysis.

Explore
Similar to 'examine'. It means investigate, delve into, question.

Illustrate
It does not mean 'draw a picture'! It means describe or show, e.g. 'Illustrate the main causes of post-natal depression'.

Interpret
E.g.'What is your interpretation of the term "immortality"?' You are being asked for your opinion. The examiner wants to see how you have developed your ability to reason and present arguments.

Justify
E.g. 'Justify the argument that 17 years of Tory rule have morally bankrupted the nation'. You are being asked to defend the statement presented. The examiner wants to know how good and reasoned an argument you can make.

Outline
This is a request to state briefly and clearly the main points of a

topic without straying into argument, discussion, debate etc. It should not be just a list: it should be a definite attempt at 'no-frills' prose.

Review

To review something (as in a theatre or book review) means to make a critical examination of something.

Significance

You are being asked to find the level of importance of a subject, e.g. 'What is the significance of Picasso's Blue Period?'

Summarise

A request to précis information into a concise description of main points, e.g. 'Summarise the main requirements for the successful cultivation of standard roses'.

Trace

Another form of investigation. You are usually being asked to explain the development of a topic from the beginning, e.g. 'Trace the growth in teenage crime in the 1980s'.

15 Troubleshooting: problems have solutions

However well organised you are, problems will crop up from time to time during your studies, particularly if you are also working and/or looking after a family. Don't panic; there is always something you can do to remedy or ease the situation.

Try to isolate the cause of any problems and deal with it, practically and emotionally, as quickly as possible.

The most important thing is to communicate. If you have a problem, be honest with yourself and recognise it. Then communicate it as quickly as possible – to your tutor, your boss or your family. Don't wait until the situation becomes chronic. Bottling things up and battling on alone is counter-productive in the long-run.

Use the following problem/solution scenarios to help you assess and deal with any difficulties you may experience while studying. Sometimes problems have a single cause and are simply solved; others are many-faceted and require more than one step to be taken to solve or ameliorate them.

Problem: I'm not enjoying my course

Solution 1: You may not have done enough research on courses available and specifically on the contents of the one you have embarked upon. See your tutor immediately and talk it over. You may need to think about changing courses altogether. This is usually possible early on in a course, so if you have reservations, communicate them early.

Solution 2: If may just be that you are not enjoying the content of a particular subject area or module within the course. Keep working, get extra help if necessary (see Chapter 12), and give yourself a treat when you've completed the section!

Solution 3: You may have embarked on a distance-learning course which involves studying alone. Some people are not cut out for lone study (look at Chapter 5). If this is the case, it may be better to abandon the course until your circumstances allow you to embark on a course at a college or university. Again talk to your tutor. Or you may just need time studying with others (see Chapter 6).

Solution 4: Stress may be preventing you working well and enjoying your studies. Stress manifests itself in many forms, so read the section on stress in Chapter 3, try to pinpoint what factor is causing your stress, and deal with it as quickly as possible. A build-up of stress over time is very damaging.

Solution 5: Having 'tested the water', it may be that studying at this level is not for you. Talk this over at length with your tutor. The last resort is to leave the course altogether, and occasionally that is the right step to take. You may be one of those people who are happier finding a job and training while you work. If so, don't feel guilty. Accept the situation and get on with your life.

Problem: I don't have enough time to study

Solution 1: You may not be managing your time effectively. Read the guidance in Chapter 4. Set priorities and see if you can organise your time better.

Solution 2: If you are also working and/or looking after a family, you need to organise and allocate time to study very carefully. Talk things over with your boss, colleagues, flatmates or family. They may need to adjust their demands on you and offer you more support and therefore time to study.

Solution 3: If you are working full-time, investigate the possibility of going part-time (if you can afford it) while you are studying.

Solution 4: If you are working, ask if you can take some time off (as paid or unpaid holiday leave) to catch up with your studies.

Solution 5: Your attitude to your studies may be at fault. Check the advice in Chapters 1 and 3. Are you really motivated and committed to your course? If not, it's the easiest thing in the world not to find time to work! If this is the case, leave the course. Someone else would love your place.

Solution 6: Children or family members are or have been ill, and looking after them has eaten into your study time. This is never easy to solve, since you normally don't get advance warning. Think about this situation in advance, however, and have contingency plans in place – a supportive extended family near at hand is the best solution, or help from friends, or a child-minder you can call on. If this is impossible, speak to your tutor; it may be possible to re-jig your timetable or find ways of enabling you to catch up with your work when the family difficulties are over. If the crisis is long-term, it is often possible to defer studies for a year or so.

Problem: I'm finding the work difficult

Solution 1: Look at Chapter 12 and analyse why. If you don't understand the subject matter, tell your tutor or subject tutor. You may need extra help generally, from your subject tutor, other students, or even a private tutor for a while. On the other hand, you may just need guidance with a particular area you're finding difficult.

Solution 2: If you don't know where to start your work, you have become disorganised; good organisation is the key to successful and effective study. Check out Chapter 2 on organising the basics, Chapter 7 on taking notes, Chapter 8 on research, Chapter 9 on storing and retrieving information, and get your act together!

Solution 3: If you are finding it difficult to get down to work your concentration may be poor; a variety of factors can cause this. Look at Chapter 3, pin down the cause, talk it over and work towards a solution.

Problem: I can't remember things

Solution 1: You may have a poor memory; many of us do, particularly as we get older. Use the memory tips and tricks in Chapter 11. Remember, too, that tiredness, illness, stress and even hunger can cause your memory to fail, so put these things right if they are causing or contributing to the problem.

Solution 2: You may not be taking adequate notes or transcribing them soon enough after a lecture. Look at Chapter 7 on effective note-taking.

Solution 3: Your research methods may need honing, particularly if this is your first experience of research-based work. Read Chapter 8.

Problem: I lack confidence

Solution: Look at Chapter 3. A lack of confidence is common in those returning to study after years away, so take heart. Talk to your tutor; this may be just a temporary phase. If not, seek professional advice. If lack of confidence is caused by problems in your personal life, talk to your family, friends or your student counsellor, and try to find a solution. Communicating your fear is half the battle.

Problem: I am afraid of failing

Solution: Rationalise your fear by talking it over, with your tutor, family and friends. If the problem is deep-rooted, seek advice from your doctor.

Problem: I can't find my notes/research papers/files

Solution 1: You haven't got the basics right (see Chapter 2). Make sure you have a permanent place to work away from distractions, where your papers will be undisturbed, all your materials are to hand, and you have a place to store your files.

Solution 2: You are not storing your papers efficiently. This is vital, not an optional extra. Look at the advice in Chapter 9 on information storage and retrieval, and make sure you number your notes/papers and file them each day. Keep up your index; keep back-up computer disks; keep hard copy back-up to computer disks; and keep up your bibliography and card index system of research sources.

Problem: I can't read my lecture notes/follow my research notes

Solution: Effective note-taking and research should underpin your studies. Read Chapters 7 and 8, and start as you mean to go on!

Problem: I find it hard to structure my essays and written assignments

Solution: Those returning to study after years away may find this problematic. These are skills you need to develop. Follow the advice in Chapter 10 and set yourself guidelines from the very beginning. You will build your skills up as you progress through the course.

Problem: I find presentations difficult and daunting

Solution: Again, for those returning to study after time away this may be uncharted territory, for it is only in fairly recent years that presentations have become an established part of course work. You need to acquire the skills to present material using visual aids. Follow the advice in Chapter 10 and put the tips into practice. Presentations will become much less daunting as your skills improve.

Problem: I find it hard to study on my own

Solution: This may come particularly hard if you are returning to study after time off working and/or bringing up a family. Read the advice in Chapter 5, especially if you are considering taking a distance learning course. If may not be for you.

Problem: I find shared study difficult

Solution: If you prefer to study alone and find it effective, that's fine. On the other hand, you may find working with others helpful at certain points in your course (see Chapter 6). Teamwork also develops skills that you may find useful during and after your course. Remember, however, that your primary objective is success. Organise your studies in the way that is most effective and successful for you.

Problem: I don't know where to start with my revision

Solution: Revision should be continuous. Chapter 13 has lots of advice on how to organise revision to make the best use of it and your time. Effective revision, like all the elements of successful study, means deciding your objectives and setting targets, priorities and schedules, so you can work towards your goal.

Problem: exams terrify me!

Solution: No one likes them, but your objective must be to arrive for your examinations relaxed and in a confident state of mind – which means careful planning. Check out Chapter 14 for guidance on how to prepare for exams and achieve your very best when you sit them.

Notes

Index